Back on Course

GAVIN & PATTI MacLEOD

WITH MARIE CHAPIAN

Back on Course

Fleming H. Revell Company
Old Tappan, New Jersey

ISBN 0-8007-1533-0

Copyright © 1987 by Gavin and Patti MacLeod
Published by the Fleming H. Revell Company
Old Tappan, New Jersey 07675
Printed in the United States of America

PATTI

I dedicate this book

To my mother and daddy, Peggy and Lee Kendig, who loved me and gave me life.

To my children—Tommy, Stephanie, and Drew Steele—who love me and gave me a meaning for my life.

To my husband, Gavin, who loves me and forced me to search for my life.

To Jesus Christ, who *is* my Love and my Life.

GAVIN

I did not want to write this book! It has not been an experience without pain. The only motivation to open and share *my* wounds is the hope that perhaps the *reader* may realize that whatever pain he or she may be experiencing *can be overcome!*

My intention is not to hurt anyone. In fact, I have attempted to protect those who have been a part—large or small—of my life.

There are many things I wish had never happened, but they did happen—and I am a living product of those experiences.

God knows my heart and my mistakes. It is *His* understanding, love, and forgiveness that is most important in my life.

This book is dedicated to my wife and to my family. In spite of everything, they are still there for me.

Thank You, God!

CONTENTS

INTRODUCTION

When "The Mary Tyler Moore Show" ended in 1977 after episode 168, there weren't floods of tears on the set because most cast members looked forward to new jobs in new shows. Valerie Harper had her own series, "Rhoda," Ted Knight was going to play in a new CBS sitcom, and Ed Asner was launching a sixty-minute series based on his Lou Grant character. Betty White had a new show lined up, with Georgia Engel in second billing. Mary herself was branching out into movies and other TV work. Gavin MacLeod, the show's lovable but melancholy newswriter, Murray, had several reasonable offers, but had no show of his own lined up yet.

Gavin's personal life was also in constant flux. He and his second wife, Patti, were moving again—this time to the eighteenth floor of a luxury condominium complex on Ocean Avenue in Santa Monica. They had moved seven times in the years they had been together. "If we're not in escrow, we're not content," Gavin joked to his friends. Sometimes, however, he wondered if they'd ever be content.

Jay Sandrich, the resident director, said, "Not one of us believes he will ever again be part of something as special." Even though they knew they'd have other shows, "The Mary Tyler Moore Show" would always remain in the hearts of the cast as the ideal show with the ideal cast, writers, and production team.

There was little time for Gavin to shed tears. He was rehearsing for *Annie Get Your Gun* with Debbie Reynolds and reading scripts for new TV sitcoms, searching for another winner. He and Patti were immersed in numerology and astrology and figuring out their stars. He was determined not to let his fears overtake him and to utilize all his creative forces to stay buoyant and happy.

After the final taping of "The Mary Tyler Moore Show," he was in his dressing room at Studio City, putting his things in a trunk to take home, when Mary's manager came in and said, dolefully, "Gavin, I'm so sorry. What are you going to do now?"

Gavin responded, "Don't you understand? I loved the series and it was great, but now it's over. I'm gonna fly like a bird!" He was being characteristically optimistic. All his life he had never looked back. A difficult childhood had made him a Today Right Now kind of person. He wouldn't let himself get uptight or depressed when things went wrong. He always wanted to be happy and to have happy people around him. When they weren't, he used his own willpower. People in Hollywood often didn't understand him—he was too lighthearted. Some thought he was weird, overly optimistic, and Gavin wondered if they didn't want to take some of his joy away from him. He and Patti, however, tried almost frantically to be happy.

When Gavin read for *Annie Get Your Gun* in the spring of 1977, he was offered the role of Sitting Bull, the Sioux

Indian chief. "They must know I'm part Indian," Gavin mused. (His father was a Chippewa Indian.) But Gavin wanted the role of fast-talking Charlie Davenport. He wanted to sing "There's No Business Like Show Business," and he wanted to let loose in the production numbers. The sedentary TV Murray wanted to *fly*.

But then in March Gavin received a call from his agent, who told him Aaron Spelling, who was producing the hit "Charlie's Angels," was launching a new series called "The Love Boat." There were other offers for roles in at least four TV series, but Gavin didn't approve of any of them. "Too violent," he said. "What's happening with television? Where are the choices? Violence? Murders? Mysteries? Detectives? Are heavies the only offers?"

His agent told him it wasn't like that. "I'm sending over a pilot script, Gavin. Read it. It's called 'The Love Boat.' "

Neither Gavin nor Patti dreamed that their marriage and their lives were gradually drifting off course. They had always been searchers and dreamers whose dreams painted over harsh realities. How could anything go wrong in Dream Land? This was Hollywood. Wasn't this supposed to be happy ever after?

. . . Almost.

Back
on
Course

PART ONE

GAVIN

I remember a windy autumn day in Pleasantville, New York, in 1935. I was four or five years old. Kids were playing on the sidewalks and jumping up the steps of the apartment buildings, down to the curb, back up again, and to the edge of the street. I was coming around the corner up the hill on Lincoln Avenue on a red scooter, zipping straight toward them, pushing with one foot and coasting down the hill, hunched low, flying. It was a gray afternoon, around supper time.

Then I caught sight of the body in the gutter.

"Hey, Allan, isn't that your grandpa?" one of the kids called out to me.

"He's drunk!"

"Shut up," I told them.

"Drunk in the street!"

And then the laughter. I could hear it all the way down the street to my father's gas station.

In 1935 business was poor for the station in a town with a population of four thousand. The country was sunk in the depression, and there were more charge customers than paying ones. My father, George See, a Chippewa

17

Indian, had a fifth-grade education, but he was a good mechanic and if the times had been better, maybe he could have made a profitable go of things. The two pumps in front of the homely brick building looked like sad cactus plants in the middle of a desert. Inside I could hear the raucous voices of the men, the rattling of their laughter. They were unshaven, rowdy, drinking men in faded shirts that always looked gray with dust; they smelled of sweat and beer. They hung around the gas station, drinking until late at night, while their wives were at home taking care of the kids.

I tugged at my father's arm. "Come help Grandpa!" It was a foolish request. One drinking man couldn't be of much help to another drunk man, and when I saw my father's condition, I recoiled instantly. Even at age four I already knew I'd be in trouble if I stayed around. The men continued their loud talking and laughing as if I weren't there.

There were lots of nights when I lay in bed trying to forget the sight of my grandfather lying in the street or my father fighting with my mother. Sometimes I'd listen to my mother's and Aunt Hazel's voices in the kitchen.

"So drunk they had to carry him home—"

"—broke the lamp and threw the ashtray at the wall—"

"—when the police came—"

So many of my nightmares were waking ones, listening to the troubling voices coming from the kitchen at night.

I lay in the darkness on my bed by the one window in the room and stared outside at the branches of the lone tree between the apartment buildings, imagining being a pirate, a sea captain, a soldier—because I knew I could dream a better life than the one I knew.

My mother nearly died giving birth to me and often

talked about it. I could hear the women's voices floating from the kitchen over the smells of Borax, Airwick, and my dad's tar soap.

"Allan was the rough one. Nearly killed me. I don't know *when* I'll get my health back."

Sometimes I had horrible dreams in which I was the cause of her death. So I preferred daydreams.

Behind our apartment building, a long hill sloped upward, backdropping a narrow, sagging row of garages. Atop the hill were the railroad tracks and magically, every night at 6:16, the New York commuter rattled past, drowning out every other sound in the world. I rushed outside to watch the magnificent giant cars sway past, rumbling and clacking along the tracks, and I'd vow, "Someday I'll ride in a train. Someday I'll go someplace special." I could see the dozing forms of businessmen in their seats in the passenger cars. Then I'd watch the caboose vanish in the distance, the empty rails still humming. For years after, I believed traveling meant going to happier places.

My mother became terribly upset when I went near the tracks. She could always find me because of my full head of blond curls. One day she entered my photograph, with my big blue eyes and blond curly hair, in the New York *Daily Mirror* "Charming Child Contest," and I won! The neighbor ladies thought I was adorable and plied me with cookies and other treats from their kitchens and candy bowls.

One of our neighbors was a man named Sylvester (or Vet, as they called him) Fowler. He was my dad's drinking buddy and best friend. Mrs. Fowler had a big heart for kids, especially for me. She knew what life was like in our house. She seemed to understand my wide-eyed, nervous expressions. She fed me cookies and let me sit in the window staring out at the street when I "ran away from home" to her house.

Our family also included my mother's brother, Jim. I called him Uncle "Bimmy." He shared a bedroom with my brother, Ronnie, and me and was a gentle, fun person. We loved him for his sense of humor and kindness to us.

Sunday mornings there were church expeditions with Mom. Bathed the night before in cold water, we wore our clean clothes and polished shoes to attend mass in the Catholic church. And Sunday afternoons the family scrambled into the Ford with my father at the wheel for our excursion through Westchester County.

We would visit our great-grandparents, Grandpa and Grandma Erickson, who owned a sprawling farm in Chappaqua. At one time Grandpa See owned a beautiful home of his own in exclusive Briarcliff Manor. He lost it through gambling and booze. Ritualistically my mother would insist we drive past the house and she would lament, "We could be living there now. Boys, that could be *your* yard. . . ."

My great-grandparents had a produce stand at the side of the road and sold lettuce, tomatoes, green peppers, and all kinds of fruit and vegetables. People drove all the way up from New York City to buy produce from their stand. My brother, Ronnie, and I would pick cherries from the cherry trees and play with their few farm animals.

Money was scarce, and people weren't paying their gasoline accounts. They'd drive their cars up to the two Shell pumps at my father's station and call out, "Fill 'er up, George." After he did they'd say, "I'll pay you next month." But they didn't pay next month. So some Sundays Dad would allow me to go with him and we'd drive to the homes of his customers and ask for the money owed him. I saw the frustration on his face and the sad sloping of his shoulders when he couldn't collect. He was a tall, strong man with sharp features, brooding eyes, ruddy complexion, and a wonderful smile. When he wasn't drinking, he was handsome. He could also be gentle and kind, a generous man who would "give the shirt off his back to you," Mom always said. Yet when he was drunk, he would attack the dust on the wall if he had a mind to.

Then one day a horrible thing happened that affected all our lives. The story went that Vet Fowler had returned home from a routine visit to the doctor, to the smell of Mrs. Fowler's soup simmering on the stove, with the dreaded news he had cancer. It was almost dinner time when Mrs. Fowler gave him a kiss and, stunned at his news, watched him leave by the kitchen door. She didn't see the gun in his hand. He got into his pickup truck and drove to a grassy spot on the parkway in Briarcliff, inserted the muzzle of the gun into his mouth, and pulled the trigger.

When my father heard about it, he fell apart. He wept like a baby—I had never seen my father cry before. I watched him sobbing and, not knowing what to do, left him alone and hovered graven-faced and frightened with Mom and Ronnie in the parlor.

The news shook the neighborhood. There was a bar next to the gas station and behind it the men would pitch horseshoes. They smoked cigars and drank beer out of cardboard containers. They talked about Vet Fowler and tried to make jokes about their experiences with him. But despair clung to them all, especially my father. He became superstitious about his own death. Vet had been only thirty-seven years old when told he had cancer. In those days, cancer meant death. It was a shadow of gloom over all of us.

Dad spent more time in the bar and Ronnie and I were often sent to coax him home. If he was in a good mood, he'd order some pig's knuckles or get us each a dill pickle out of the wooden pickle barrel at the door. We'd sit with him and drink Coca-Cola from cups and eat potato chips out of a box. The potato chips were fresh and salty, and sitting there with Dad when he was not yet drunk enough to be ugly, I felt a tenderness toward him. It was rare and special.

My mother, Margaret Shea See, was a beautiful lady of Swedish and Irish descent, a hardworking woman who did her best to take care of us. She was born, raised, and married in the Pleasantville area and never traveled farther away than a hundred miles in any direction. She rarely got to New York City, only thirty miles to the south.

I had always tried to please Mom, and Dad, too, but I couldn't seem to get his approval. He made me feel as if I had done something wrong—as if I wasn't good enough. The men at the station referred to children as "rug rats," and I figured that's what Dad thought of me.

When I was older I tried to get Dad's attention by playing the drums, but there was always that edge of disapproval. In those days men had their pals; children and wives were something else. A man took care of them but didn't get involved in their personal lives. I think my father thought a good woman was one who didn't nag or get in a man's way or try to change him. She took care of the kids and didn't put a man down for his friends and how he spent his time. A good woman was there to help him get into the house if he was too drunk to get up the stairs. She would come to bail him out of jail, clean him up if he got into a fight, but she should never harp on it the next day. She cooked and cleaned, had babies, and didn't bother him with domestic trivialities. If the kids were sick, she shouldn't bother him with it. She shouldn't spend much money and shouldn't nag him about how he spent money.

And to women, drinking husbands were like naughty little boys and treated much like paying boarders who sometimes became ruling tyrants and treated their wives and families like hired help.

My mother had a seventh-grade education and was one of those women. She was close to her hardworking mother, who also was married to an alcoholic, my grandfather Shea. Mom demonstrated her love to us by taking care of our physical needs; she did the laundry and sewing, she bandaged cuts and scratches, and plied fevers with aspirin and sore throats with glasses of warm salt water. She learned to drive when she was sixteen and happily delivered us boys wherever we wanted to go. She came to every game, recital, play, and spelling bee. She stitched Boy Scout badges onto our ironed khaki uniform shirts, baked cookies for Valentine's Day parties at school, and never forgot a single vaccination or booster shot. We wanted hugs and praise, but it was hot meals and clean clothes we had to settle for.

And there was always food. I ate ravenously of the food that represented her love. Meatballs, potato soup, potato pancakes, *kages, brods*, cookies, and puddings. I grew stout like my mother and grandmother. Eventually the kids in the neighborhood nicknamed me "Tubber." Ronnie, who had been thin and sickly most of his young life, eventually became "Tubber-Two."

As I grew older, my interests and dreams were so unlike

those of the rest of the family that I began to feel alienated and different. I loved music and art and hated the gas station. I loved to read plays out loud and hated fighting and violence. I could talk to my Aunt Sis about plays and movie stars, but nobody else in the family seemed to love those things the way I did. I won a scholarship to an art school in Chicago when I was nine, but my father wouldn't hear of my going.

"Art school? That's crazy. I never heard of anything so dumb for a boy," he said. "Margaret, what are you trying to do to him?"

"He's got art talent, George. He's a very good drawer."

"That's dumb."

So I didn't go to art school.

As much as I feared my father, I also feared losing him. I never forgot overhearing him talking to my mother one shadowy afternoon when I was about eleven.

"I'm going to die young, Peg."

"George! What are you talking about?"

"I can feel it. I'm going to die young, like Vet Fowler did."

"Don't talk like that."

"He got cancer at thirty-seven and—"

"And killed himself, that's what he did."

"Died at thirty-seven."

"Are you planning on *shooting* yourself, George?"

"I just got a feeling I'm gonna die young of cancer."

You heard so many frightening stories in those days; people going off to war never to return, getting killed driving and drinking, or committing suicide.

Why couldn't things be *nice?*

I took refuge in make-believe. I acted out stories like the ones I saw in the movies. These were happy stories, not stories of killing and dying. Saturday was the best day of the week for me because I went to the movies. After I finished my chores at home (cleaning the basement, sweeping, hauling in the coal, and running errands), with seven cents to get into the movies and an extra dime for Jujubies and popcorn, I was off for the rest of the day. I'd stay at the theatre watching the entire show two and three times. The only thing that drew me out was hunger. And once, when I saw a family of immigrants eating food out of a sack in a row behind me, I even wanted to do that. Mom was horrified at the idea.

"Those people probably have no home, Allan. You have a home. You'll eat your supper at home, not like a poor, starving immigrant."

The idea that there were people poorer than we were worried me. Some days Mom drove to the Catholic church to bring food, and I helped take care of the wartime victory garden so we could give some of the food to desperate families. I always cleaned my plate because my mother reminded me of all the hungry people who would be grateful to get what we got to eat.

Mealtimes were not peaceful times, however. As I grew older, Dad complained about my habits and behavior to my mother.

"What do you want him to do, play Ping-Pong all his life?"

"I don't want him playing football anymore. It's a dangerous sport. He could get hurt or killed, God forbid."

"How long you gonna baby that boy?"

Dinner was always tense. My father could be riled into a fury if the foods on his plate touched. The lima beans couldn't touch the potatoes and the gravy on the meat loaf couldn't seep onto the potatoes or the lima beans. If the foods ran into one another, he cursed angrily, causing a commotion. Finally, Mother bought him a plastic sectioned plate like the ones used in institutions, and this quieted him.

"Maybe the kid likes to go fishing—"

"Allan has band practice now."

"Maybe he doesn't want to practice those drums— maybe he'd rather go fishing!"

I had been fishing with Dad and his buddies a few times. No great thrill. I'd squeeze into the car, crushed between the men, breathing their beer fumes and cigarette smoke and listening to their bad jokes. I never knew when their lighthearted drinking would evolve into drunken ugliness. The trip might begin with jolly insults and ribald tales and gradually become hateful attacks, filthy stories, and fierce arguments. The slightest gesture of antagonism could set one of the men off like a lighted firecracker. I guess I lived with so much yelling that I learned to tune out and ignore it.

To my father, fishing meant drinking. So while he drank, I fished. At the end of the day, Dad would pay me a dollar for the fish I caught and he'd bring it home to Mom. It was our little secret.

After these fishing expeditions, the band of drunken men went home to fight with their wives. One night I was awakened to screaming. I rushed into the kitchen in time to see my father staggering toward my mother with a carving knife. I dove between them, catching my father off guard, and was able to wrench the knife out of his hand.

The next day my mother wouldn't say a word about the episode. It was as though it had never happened. She denied, and I denied. We both preferred fantasy, perhaps.

My grandfather was an alcoholic, too. When my mother was called to help in the "family emergencies," meaning my grandfather was drunk, she often took me with her in the car. I'd sit outside waiting for her, listening to the battle going on inside. Finally there'd be the whine of the police siren, and then the swaying form of my grandfather would be guided down the steps into the police car. I vowed I'd never be like him—and I'd never be like my father.

My grandfather was the worst drunk of them all, in my opinion, because he was cruel. He liked making jokes at the expense of others, like the time he gave me a dog biscuit and told me it was a cookie, then watched me happily eat it in front of a whole group of people.

But then something amazing happened. When another uncle of mine, Uncle Johnny, went to war, my grandfather made a prayer to God which the whole family knew about. He prayed and told God that if He would see to it his son came home from the war unhurt, he would quit drinking forever. Here's the shock: his son came home unhurt and Grandpa *did* quit drinking. Uncle Bimmy joked that

Grandpa was the first man in the family to quit drinking: "It could give us a bad name!"

In the midst of the commotion going on around me, I listened to the opera on Saturdays. I couldn't tell a soul how enthralled I was because I didn't think they'd understand. I didn't know *anyone* else who listened to opera. I practiced my drums and loved playing in the marching band. It was the best thing that could have happened to me in the ninth grade. I became a member of the largest military all-male marching band in the state of New York. I also started my own band, and we played for school dances. I had dreams of being a great drummer one day.

I'll never forget the tender moments: the times when my father would lean across the front seat of the car toward Mom on our Sunday drives and sing, "When your hair has turned to silver, I will love you just the same," and she would smile at him and sigh, "Oh, George, that's my favorite song." Those moments were what I wanted all the time. Happy. Sweet. Uncomplicated.

One day the band played at a football game, and my father showed up. He hadn't been feeling well and was walking with a cane. I could see him out of the corner of my eye, wearing his striped pants and white shirt. I walked tall and proud so my father could see me drumming. I wondered if he felt proud or if he would rather have seen me on the field playing football.

The cane didn't go away. When hard times forced my father to give up the gas station, he took a job driving a gas truck.

He hated doctors and refused to see one, no matter how sick he was. If he was sick, he tried to ignore it as long as he could. Mom would practically have to corral him to find out how he felt. As long as he was able to get around, he believed he was okay. But one day in the late fall of 1944, Mom knew something was seriously wrong. She got him in the car and drove him to the doctor's office. He still insisted he'd be fine.

I came home from school that day to find the house empty. My mother was always home, but this day she wasn't. Neither was my father. I paced the rooms. At six o'clock the telephone rang, and I answered it. "Mom! Where are you?"

Without a beat of hesitation, the voice on the telephone announced, "Allan, the doctor says your father is dying of cancer and has six months to live. Run across the tracks and tell your aunt and uncle."

I stood frozen in place, unable to move or speak. For many years after, the sound of a telephone was like the voice of death to me, and for a long time I refused to answer one.

My father stayed in the hospital for an operation called a colostomy, in which the colon is removed. I took extra jobs mowing lawns and helping builders carry lumber and pour cement.

When Dad came home, Ronnie and I lay awake listening to him cry in pain. I prayed that God would help him. And then I prayed that he would die, just to end his agony.

My father had been a strapping, strong man of 185 pounds. Now he slowly lost more and more weight. He had cobalt treatments, and we were all hopeful, but he became weaker.

We had a little white dog named Suzie he liked to take for walks, but one day he had no strength to walk.

Then the ambulance came to take him back to the hospital.

One last gesture Dad made toward Ronnie and me was to arrange for a box of potato chips to be at his bedside because he knew we liked them. Mom would scold him, "You're not going to try to eat these, are you, George?"

She didn't understand that it was his way of reaching out to his sons. "Of course not—they're for the boys. They like them."

Dad died on June 11, 1945, at the age of thirty-nine. He was buried in his only suit and carried in the hearse I had cleaned out and washed many times at his station. It was a big funeral, the biggest in town, they said; even the rich people from the other side of the tracks came. There was lots of food and people were kind to Mom and Ronnie and me.

I remember the words of the priest: "Let not your heart be troubled: ye believe in God, believe also in me. In my Father's house are many mansions: if it were not so, I would have told you. I go to prepare a place for you" (John 14:1, 2).

My heart was troubled. "Am I to blame for his death because I prayed You'd take him to end his suffering? Is my father in a mansion in heaven now?"

I wept when I looked at him. His face was still and hard. I felt a shudder go through my body. I had never heard him say *I love you*.

Acting, it turned out, became my way to gain attention and approval. Even at four years old, I loved the fun and attention of being on the stage. (It was at this tender age I made my theatrical debut as a bear whose gift to the world was to give bear hugs.) Later I was in every program and stage presentation in grade school, and when a children's theatre came to school with *Robin Hood*, I was captivated. I performed in *Captain Applejack*, a play about a quiet Englishman who dreams he's a pirate. It was fabulous. Those experiences showed me there was a world where I belonged.

In high school, the joyous discovery of music and theatre filled my life with creative energy, friends, and fun. One of my closest friends was a guy named Jimmy Downey. We were on the football team together until we accidentally broke a player's leg in a tackle. I was active and busy, involved in every possible school event. No longer fat and completely out of my shell, I even ventured to dream and plan for a career as a professional musician or actor.

When I heard Ithaca College had a scholarship program for theatre majors, I could hardly dare hope to qualify. My brother, Ronnie, encouraged me to try. "You can do it,

Allan. I know you can. You'll be the first in the family to
go to college."

I summoned the courage and applied. After the audition I felt good, like a real actor. But still I was certain a
theatrical scholarship was only a dream. Then one day a
few weeks later, I was coming home from my part-time
job when I saw Ronnie running toward me across the
vacant lot and over the hill behind our house. He was
excited and waving a piece of paper in the air. "You made
it! You made it!" he shouted. "They accepted you!"

We had always heard poor kids like us don't get to go to
college. But I'd prove the people who said that were wrong.
I worked all the harder, making extra money. Even with
the scholarship it would be hard. We had no money for
food or books, so I took another job for my Uncle Harry on
his garbage truck, picking up garbage ($2.50 an hour and
all you can eat, he would joke).

Finally, I said good-bye to family and friends in Pleasantville and headed north to Ithaca College. I was just sixteen
years old. My friend Jim Downey, who would later run
the famous Downey's Steak House on Eighth Avenue in
New York, wrote in my high school yearbook, "Five minutes till curtain, Mr. See." Jim Downey was one of my
greatest supporters. He always believed I would do something terrific. ("After all, you broke a leg for *real*," he
laughed.) It was 1947. America was in an optimistic mood.

A friend at Ithaca College, Lou Gallo, two years my
senior, arranged for me to stay in his boarding house,
owned by a kindly older lady named Mrs. Frith. Even
though I had managed to save some money the summer
before I left for college by working on the garbage truck
and doing odd jobs, I was still short of money. In order to
pay for food, I got a job in the school cafeteria.

I never liked cliques or social fraternities. In high school I shied away from being part of the "in" crowd and tried to be friendly to everyone. I wanted everyone included. Jimmy Downey once said, "Allan loves the whole world. You could be the gangster John Dillinger, and he'd offer to take you home to meet his mom and have Sunday dinner." In college I joined the fraternity of Theta Alpha Phi, the national honorary dramatic fraternity, and eventually became its vice-president. Members were elected on the basis of their acting ability, personal character, and academic rating. It was open to anyone, and nobody could blackball you.

My first play was a workshop production of *Salome*, directed by Richard Woods, who went on to become a successful New York actor. The year was 1949. I played a small part in the production and apparently had a glaring effect on Miss Lear, the speech teacher.

"Your speech is terrible, Allan," she told me.

"It is?"

"Yes. In order to do the classics, you must work on diction, elocution, projection—"

"Oh, I do all that."

"You have an *accent*, Allan."

"*Me?* An accent?"

"Yes, and you're going to have to do a lot of work on it, beginning with phonetics."

"I don't think I have an accent."

Though I think of myself as a natural comedian, my first roles were in serious plays like *Julius Caesar*, in which I carried a spear and had one line: "Hail, Caesar."

Thirty years later, before 43 million television viewers each week, my character of newswriter Murray Slaughter got along fine with lines like, "Aw, come on, Mair, that's tar*iffick*." But I knew Miss Lear was right. "Hay-el, Ceesah" just wouldn't do.

"All right, Allan, let's give it another try. Listen and repeat. Puh—puh—puh—repeat."

"—per—per—"

"Once more. Listen and repeat. Puh—puh—puhrfect."

"Puh—puh. Puh—*poifect*."

I began inviting fellow students to my room at Mrs. Frith's to read plays aloud. Long into the night hours we could be heard emoting away. It started with meeting once a week, and then we read together more and more, as we gained confidence. We figured genius has to start somewhere. Lou Gallo was there, and Jan Peters, Mort Clark, Nick DeMarco, Ronnie Pedrone, and John Bartholomew Tucker. They are all successful now. Today Nick is in advertising in New York, John Bartholomew is a popular personality and voice-over on radio and TV, and Lou Gallo is a producer. Mort Clark is a professor of drama and Jan Peters is an educator and actor.

School acting classes were beginning to help me become freer to express my feelings. I had the idea that to be accepted I had to be happy all the time. But I was learning the world wouldn't reject me if I said the wrong thing or didn't smile twenty-four hours a day. It was still difficult for me to express negative feelings. I dreaded ugly scenes, fighting, and the ultimate pain these emotional outbursts represented. To me getting angry, even on stage, meant violence. Expressing displeasure toward someone could mean a battle. So I kept a cheerful face and tried to enjoy the world around me. That was fine, but denial of problems, I would discover, is not.

On most weekends I went home to Pleasantville, hitching a ride from Jan in his 1933 Chevy. I worked for Uncle

Harry on the garbage truck to earn some money. I'd pick up the garbage at a friend's house with a hat pulled over my eyes in the daytime, and that night I'd be back to the same house all dressed up for a party.

We had to move from our house on Sarles Lane after Dad died. Mom and Ronnie were now living in a smaller place on Ossining Road. I paid visits to aunts and grandparents when I was home. Once I had an encounter with my mother's father, whose very presence used to terrify me when I was younger. The old man sat opposite me in his reclining chair wearing slippers with no socks, his chin on his chest, peering at me over his glasses. The same man whom my mother had to call the police for because of his drunken violence. The same man who quit drinking because his son was spared.

"What are you studying up there in that college?"

"Theatre."

"Huh?"

"I'm studying Theatre. I'm going to be an actor."

"You're going to *college* and you're studying *Theatre?*"

"Yeah. That's right."

(Silence.)

"They teach that up there? Well, if that isn't something. What do you plan on doing when you get out?"

"I want to be an actor."

His face lit up.

"Good for you. Listen, sonny, whatever you want to do, *you do it.*"

I was stunned. I didn't expect that kind of affirmation from anyone in the family.

"—and don't you *ever* let anybody talk you out of what you want to do."

I wondered, *Does this mean my grandpop likes me?*

I would stop at the drugstore and buy my mother her favorite perfume, Evening in Paris, on my way back home. She was always delighted.

"Oh, Allan. Your father always bought me Evening In Paris."

In her mind Dad was a hero who sang "When Your Hair Has Turned to Silver" to her and presented her with oceans of little blue bottles of Evening in Paris.

I saw my grandparents on my father's side, too. They lived in three tiny, airless rooms above the drugstore next to the Catholic church. "And to think we're Episcopalian," Grandmother despaired. To visit them, I'd duck into the door next to the drugstore and hurry up the stairs before anyone on the street saw me. I thought that where a person lived was important. Rich people lived in better homes, and I thought maybe it was because they were better people. For most of my life I would have the idea a big house was the sign of a good, successful person. I felt guilty for being ashamed of my family and wished I could be proud of who I was and where I came from.

Sitting in my grandparents' hot, dreary living room, which smelled of bacon grease, was a graceless experience. At college I lied and told friends the publisher of *See* magazine was my uncle and that my family was from Briarcliff and very rich.

My Uncle Harry, who owned the garbage business, was becoming an unmanageable drunk. Eventually the booze dissipated him and he sold the business and moved to Florida, where he bought a liquor store. One night some men came in and robbed him and beat him up. He died not long after that.

While home, I not only visited my family, I also took long walks. I liked to walk around the house of Judson

Laire, who I thought was the most famous person living in Pleasantville at the time. Judson Laire played "Papa" on "I Remember Mama" on television during the show's run from 1949 to 1956. I would squint my eyes at the big, old Victorian house on the other side of the tracks and think, *An* actor *lives in that house.*

As I walked, I recited Shakespeare to practice diction, all the way to Thornwood, through town, past the cemetery. I stopped reciting when I got to the cemetery and I whistled instead. Then past the dump, where I could still see the men of the town who, in the depression years, skinned the animals they trapped there and hung the little pink bodies up on sticks . . . and up the hill to the left where the trees were thick and rocks big enough to sit on were strewn. There, sitting alone on a rock, with only the sound of the wind, I would read aloud: "To-morrow, and to-morrow, and to-morrow. . . ."

The leaves bristled above in the trees and a cold wind from Canada blew down. ". . . Creeps in this petty pace from day to day. . . ."

The gray light of twilight cast shadows between the trees, and I'd pull up the collar of my fake leather jacket.

And be Macbeth.

Back at Ithaca I buried myself in reading plays, learning production, and playing roles like Chekhov's *Uncle Vanya*, Desdemona's father in Shakespeare's *Othello*, Falstaff in *Henry IV Part I*, a soldier in an original play, *K.G.*, and John Owen in *The Corn Is Green*. I was popular with everyone on campus; friends were important to me and I liked being the life of the party. A bunch of us were always together driving to Taughannock Falls, going to Pennsylvania to see a Wagnerian opera, or to Binghamton for a spaghetti dinner at the home of a friend's parents. I didn't have the money to take girlfriends on expensive dates, so I discovered dates could be things like reading poetry until the light of morning, or watching the sun set over Cayuga Lake, or picking apples. There were free concerts, workshop productions of plays and musicals, fabulous walks along the Finger Lakes, and parties. I didn't drink much during those years; I was afraid. But I loved to dance and went to every dance the school sponsored.

Beatrice MacLeod, drama coach, director, and teacher, made plays explode with life and power in each of her students' hearts. She directed several productions during my years at Ithaca, including Shakespeare's *Much Ado About Nothing* and *Judgment Day* by Elmer Rice. I will never

38

forget Beatrice MacLeod. So great was her impression on me that several years after graduation, I changed my name to MacLeod. (Gavin is a name I chose after seeing an inspiring television drama entitled "Gavin." It was about a cerebral palsy victim with immense integrity.)

At graduation in June 1952, my mother said she was the proudest woman in the state of New York. Sitting on a folding chair on the lawn, she squinted in the sun to catch a glimpse of me getting my diploma. I was the first in the family to become a college graduate, a bona fide B.F.A., Bachelor of Fine Arts, and I won the Theatre Department's "Best Actor" award.

But there was a war going on in Korea and friends in my group talked about it more and more, especially with graduation and a world outside the campus facing us now. "This country is at war. Our guys are getting killed. Here we are, doing plays, learning our lines, and going to class when guys like us are right this very minute in some rice paddy facing gunfire." To me those words sounded like lines from another play. Unreal. We all had the draft staring us in the face. Driving back to Pleasantville, listening to Johnny Ray singing "The Little White Cloud That Cried," and passing through the lush, green Finger Lakes country along lazy, quiet roads, I felt that old fear. Just when you think it's going to be an okay world and you dare to reach out to it and say boldly, "All right, I'm ready to grow up," they hand you a gun and say go shoot somebody.

Later that evening I told Mom I was going to enlist in the air force. She didn't like to be demonstrative with her feelings, but she was not pleased at this news. "Oh, Allan, I hate those airplanes. Dropping bombs and all—there's nowhere to go but down. Wouldn't the navy be safer? If something happened, you could always swim. I can see you on a boat, but not in an airplane!"

In the meantime, I was still playing the drums and dreaming of forming another dance band like the one I had started in high school. I said good-bye to Mom and Ronnie once more and headed for air force basic training, which was followed by an assignment in the Public Information Office. But I also landed a spot in the U.S. Air Force Band. The bandleader was Tommy Newson, who later went on to fame on the "Tonight Show" with Johnny Carson. Tommy Newson told me at every rehearsal, "Keep the beat, just keep the beat . . ." and when we met again thirty years later in California, he greeted me, "Well, are you still keeping the beat?"

After my service duty ended, anxious to get my show-business career started, I went home to Pleasantville and told everyone, "I gotta give it a try in New York. They say New York will either make or break an actor."

"How will you live, Allan?" Mom wanted to know. Looking at her, I suddenly realized she was getting older. I had never thought of her as old. Only a few years had passed since I left home, and her hair was almost completely white. Her face was more drawn, her walk slower. She had worked as a bookkeeper in the bank ever since Dad died, never complaining about not having enough money, never once asking for help from her sons, never appearing anything but indomitable. I appreciated her pride. In her eyes her boys were perfect. I wanted to hand the world to her, give her a wonderful life of ease—sunny days by a luxurious pool—I wanted to make up for what she'd lost out on. "Mom," I said, "I'm gonna make it, and when I do, we'll all move to the other side of the tracks."

"So? You haven't told me yet how you're going to live in the city."

"I can always get a job."

"Yeah, like the soda fountain job you had at Grants," my brother laughed. "You remember, Allan—you gave some girl a free sundae, and she told the boss, and he fired you."

Mom added, "That job lasted one day."

"Wasn't too smart of the girl, was it?" I chuckled. "She could have had a free sundae every day."

We all threw back our heads and laughed. We didn't embrace, but laughter was just as good.

Then Mom repeated, "Allan, how *are* you going to live?"

"There are nine million stories in The Naked City," the narrator of the popular fifties TV series of the same name used to say. And all nine million of them must have been congregrated on Eighth Avenue and Fifty-first Street when I arrived in Manhattan on a rainy September morning in 1954. I didn't know anything about getting into the theatre, but at least I would be in the city where it all happened.

I arrived in New York City during what has been called the "faceless fifties." The theatre was suffering from "an extreme case of loss of identity." In the fifties America found its chief literary heroes in the likes of Holden Caulfield and Stanley Kowalski, and movie heroes in James Dean and others like him.

The Korean War had ended, Eisenhower was still president, and Elvis Presley was an unknown entity driving a truck in Memphis. The brooding search for identity and meaning in life was characterized by fifties poets like Allen Ginsberg, Jack Kerouac, and action painters like Jackson Pollock and Franz Kline. Countering the alienation theme were popular religious heroes such as Bishop Fulton Sheen, Norman Vincent Peale, Billy Graham, and Oral Roberts.

Glamour was passé on the New York stage. Placid cinema gods and goddesses were picking up their checks at the studio doors and exiting the Hollywood scene, and in their stead were the "raw human emotion" people. In New York "the Method" was in. Directors like Lee Strasberg and Elia Kazan, and writers like Arthur Miller and Tennessee Williams, were making theatrical history. Glitz was out. Reality was where it was at. People wanted sweat, mumbling, real guts. Out with the tinsel and glitter. On with the ugly dockside of *On the Waterfront* and torpid ghetto of *A Streetcar Named Desire*. Instead of "Tennis anyone?" and "Mother, Father, the calla lilies are in bloom" at the movies, the fans of the 1950s heard, "Charlie, oh, Charlie, you don't understand. I coulda had class. I coulda been a contender." Leading men with the characteristic impassivity of the forties Hollywood pretty men made way for the grunting, *feeling* princes of the fifties, like Marlon Brando.

Hollywood produced some fifties musicals starring Pat Boone, Doris Day, and Debbie Reynolds, which fed a need for entertainment, but it was not until *West Side Story*, *Fiddler on the Roof*, and *Sound of Music* in the sixties that the movie musical was heralded as a platform for genius. The elite audience was not looking to be entertained; they wanted to gasp, groan, sigh. Pain was more sophisticated than glitz. This was the world of show business that I wanted to break into. The question was, could I adapt to it?

My friend Vince Klemmer landed a job as an electrician at Radio City Music Hall and helped me get hired as an usher and elevator operator. My mother was so relieved she didn't mind the collect call. "So how much does it pay?"

"I went to a million employment agencies, Mom. I filled out a million applications, but nobody did cartwheels when they saw my job-experience record had been acting, drumming, mowing lawns, and picking up garbage."

"So how much are you earning?"

"It's wonderful, because Radio City Music Hall has got to be the most exciting theatre in the world! You brought me there for the first time when Ronnie and I were just little kids. Remember, Mom?"

"So how much—"

"Thirty-two dollars a week. Not including the uniform."

I walked to work to save the subway fare. Taking long strides, I could cover the distance between Seventy-fourth Street and Rockefeller Center in about half an hour. I passed the countless benches crowded with men and women holding paper bags of all their worldly possessions as they fed the pigeons; I met bedraggled panhandlers, ragged, embittered women who couldn't be as old as they looked, men with flags giving speeches, all moving on the streets and sidewalks, but seeming to stand still. I'd ease my pace at Fifty-ninth Street, slowing enough to gaze into the windows of the exclusive shops and restaurants. And I promised myself that one day I would shop at the fine men's clothing stores. I thought buying a whole box of underwear at one time was the true mark of affluence and success. Past the Plaza Hotel where the hansom cabs and their patient horses stood waiting for fares on Central Park South, with a stop at the deli on Fifty-second Street for a danish and coffee to go. I'd arrive about one minute early.

The trade paper, *Show Business*, published by Leo Schull, came out on the stands once a week. At thirty-five cents, it was a well-spent investment for an aspiring actor or actress because it listed all of the shows, producers, and directors holding auditions. I faithfully pored over its pages and circled the auditions I planned to attend. One of them was for an Off Broadway children's theatre production of the George Bernard Shaw play *Androcles and the Lion.* I auditioned and landed the unlovable part of the captain.

The company played to audiences of children who hated the character and threw things at me. Prancing across the stage in my first professional acting role, I was clobbered with everything from peanuts to milk cartons to Coke bottles by the children in the audience. The show went on tour and the troup traveled in vans and a station wagon.

By sleeping in a sleeping bag, eating only once a day, and doing my laundry in hotel sinks, I was able to pay off all my debts and save over two hundred dollars. By the time I returned to New York, I had been hit by more apple cores and heard more boos than I would ever hear the rest of my acting career. Now I had to find a new place to live, as well as another job.

My old friend Jimmy Downey was now running a restaurant on Eighth Avenue called Downey's. He gave me a job as a cashier and also let me stay in his apartment on Forty-fifth Street between Eighth and Ninth Avenues, across from the Martin Beck Theatre.

It was at this point I decided to change my name. I didn't like the jokes people made about the name *See,* and I didn't feel Allan was distinctive enough.

Mom was amazed, to put it mildly. "Your father will turn over in his grave."

"Well, Mom, I'm tired of people asking me if I'm Chinese."

"You will always be Allan George William See to me, Mister Gavin MacLeod. I will always call you Allan."

She bought me a ticket for the Easter Communion Breakfast sponsored by St. Patrick's Cathedral in Manhattan. The breakfast was held at the Waldorf Astoria and Gavin MacLeod, Professional Actor, dressed in his best clothes for the event. The only seat I could find was next to a tall, striking Radio City Music Hall Rockette named Joan Rootvik, whom everyone called "Rootie." I was immediately smitten.

Soon after we began dating, I landed a part in an Off Broadway play called *The Son-in-Law of Mr. Pear*. Bill Putch played the role of Mr. Pear, and I played his son-in-law. Bill was married to actress Jean Stapleton. He went on to found and direct a theatre in Pennsylvania called The Totem Pole Playhouse, where he directed plays for more than twenty years. Many years later Jean starred in TV's "All in the Family."

Jimmy Downey made sure I ate at least one good meal a day. Downey's Steak House was already the most popular actors' hangout in New York City and served the best hamburgers and steaks on Eighth Avenue. It was known as Sardi's Very Very West.

I auditioned as an understudy in the Broadway hit *Hatful of Rain*. The director, Frank Corsaro, who was my acting teacher, gave me an appointment to read for the understudy for Tony Franciosa's role, Polo, as well as a small part in the play. After the audition I went to work at Downey's and was at the cash register by the front door when the telephone rang with the news I'd gotten the job. I would understudy Polo and play the Man in the Hallway. I was now a Broadway actor.

Walter Lang, who directed *The King and I* at 20th Century-Fox Studios, saw me in *Hatful of Rain* and was impressed. He told the studio, "Gavin MacLeod is a combination of Richard Widmark and Yul Brynner. He's good. He's going places." The film version of *Hatful of Rain* was produced by 20th Century-Fox, but I had already signed for the road tour and wasn't able to miss performances to appear in it.

In 1955 I married Rootie, the beautiful Rockette I'd met at the Easter Communion Breakfast, and thought for sure I was the happiest guy on earth.

I looked forward to the National Road Company tour of *Hatful* and left my new wife in our New York apartment for the road. One of my friends had something to say about that. "You're making a big mistake, Gavin, if you don't mind my saying so."

"You mean going on the road?"

"No. I mean getting married. You two are worlds apart. Different types. I'm telling you, there's gonna be problems."

But I hated conflict. "Naw," I said in my most optimistic, jolly voice, "we'll work it out."

We tried. And tried. The marriage, though it lasted eighteen years, never really did "work out." Eight years of counseling didn't help, success didn't help, money didn't help, having a family of four magnificent children didn't help. To this day I wrestle with guilt over the failure of that first marriage.

When I got back to New York in 1957, following the national tour of *Hatful*, I was filled with new assurance as an actor. I had worked with the best Method performers and gained valuable experience. I had memorized every one of the male roles in the play and played them all. Now I walked with confidence up Seventh Avenue to auditions. I felt I'd paid my dues. I was even thinking of trying Hollywood.

In the spring I boarded the train for Pleasantville, and watching the silhouette of New York slip farther into the distance, I settled into my seat and thought about how I would tell my mother of my new decision to try Hollywood. Outside the window the green, awakening Hudson River Valley sprawled dew-covered and silent. The leaves were returning to the trees, and between the shaggy trunks of the silver maples I could see the flowering dogwoods' bushy heads. Plain, homely houses were strewn along the edges of the hills and alongside the railroad tracks.

Pleasantville looked drab and bleached now compared to New York City. Like every small-town boy who returns home a success, I imagined coming home to a hero's welcome, greeted by the mayor standing on a reviewing stand in the middle of Lincoln Avenue. The mayor would hold out the key to the city to me amid a throng of cheering hometowners. Posters, banners, and flags would fly, bearing slogans of praise.

Instead, I sat in the worn green chair by the window in the living room of the apartment on Ossining Road with Mom and Ron.

"I have the name of an agent in Hollywood—I mean, at least I gotta give it a try—" I began.

My mother's face was serious. "Rootie just lost a baby, Allan. The move may be hard on her. Besides, you're no Cary Grant or Clark Gable."

Though nobody called me "Tubber" anymore, I didn't think of myself as a dashing leading man. I liked character roles. "I just want to try making a go of acting, Mom. I have the name of an agent, and at least it's a start."

"But how will you live?"

Always practical. *People get that way when they work in banks,* I thought. Ron was working in the same bank with

Mom now and dating one special girl, Anna. He would get married, work at a steady job, live a good *sensible* life. I admired him.

"California is far away, Allan. How will Mom get you with the brush if you're three thousand miles away?"

I laughed. "Ron, do you remember when Grandma Shea called the police because Mom was hitting us with the brush?"

"I still have the scars."

"I never hit you *that* hard," Mom said.

"Mom, how come Dad never spanked us with the brush?" I asked.

"Yeah—he never spanked us, *period*," added Ron.

Not knowing the effect her words would have on us, she answered, "Well . . . I think he loved you too much."

Ron and I couldn't look at each other. We moved into the tiny kitchen where a fresh-baked pineapple upside-down cake waited on the table. "So, Allan? You haven't told me yet how you'll live out there in California."

"I'll get an acting job."

"Allan, you have aptitude. You could be an accountant!"

"I'm an actor, Mom."

"But it's not a steady job. People don't *stay* actors, do they? Now, accounting—there's a steady and reliable profession, Allan."

But I was searching for something else. Glory, acclaim, praise, love? Whatever it is that a dreamer wants, I wanted it.

Imagine a city strewn like a million puzzle pieces in 140 different communities across a basin of land spotted with canyons, hills, and deep valleys; illuminate this with a million vibrating klieg lights, glaring neon signs, tall, luminescent glass buildings, and ancient Spanish adobes; sprinkle it with dusty, somber palm trees, clusters of orange groves, and some oil derricks; string a tangled labyrinth of screaming, traffic-packed avenues and 11 million people in motion, and their ocean of low, flat houses, condominiums, and apartment buildings; then shroud it all under a thick, heavy, pale orange subtropical smog permanently obliterating the sky and sun; finally, wall these forty thousand square miles (as much space as the entire state of Rhode Island) with rugged mountain ranges, rolling hills, steep bluffs, and seventy-four miles of seacoast, pounding surf, and offshore islands—and you have Los Angeles.

The city known as the primary marketplace of the Pacific Coast is the focal point for one of the greatest population migrations in American history. In seventy-five years it grew to the financial epicenter of the West Coast and is home to more than twenty thousand industrial companies, trading with more than 163 nations.

The City of Angels is a sprawling megalopolis connected by more than fifteen hundred miles of freeway. It is the home of the Rose Bowl, ultramodern industrial and electronics plants, rhinestone cowboys, movie stars, real estate booms, scientific research, art, fashion, international trade, the Dodgers, Magic Mountain, and nearby Disneyland.

Into this city of dreams came Gavin MacLeod with yet one more dream to add to the already 11 million jammed between the synchronized traffic lights and suburbs, which extended sixty miles in any direction from the Civic Center downtown. To me, L.A. was Hollywood, and Hollywood *period*. With the nation's highest standard of living and thousands of starry-eyed entertainment people, young and old, pouring into the city like herring, competition was rough. It seemed that everybody was in show business. The hopeful actors and actresses worked as waiters, taxi drivers, real estate agents, clerks, secretaries, lifeguards, salespeople, janitors, cooks, maids, parking attendants—I even met a veterinarian auditioning for TV commercials. There were would-be directors, producers, agents, writers. Everybody seemed to be carrying a script under his or her arm. The sad truth was, for every two thousand people carrying scripts and collecting unemployment checks while looking for work in Hollywood, there were perhaps one hundred jobs. I was undaunted.

To me Los Angeles was a city of dreamers and doers. I saw it as one big Hollywood production full of marvelous possibilities for the future. Everybody had a dream. But not everybody goes after that dream realistically. You have to work hard, train, take classes, work harder, train—not all performers are willing to put that much into their work. Oh, Los Angeles was a culture shock all right, but very,

very exciting. I was a small-town boy from the East in glamorous "Tinseltown." I couldn't allow myself to be intimidated by the oppressive heat, the smog, the high prices, crime, crowds, and *ohhh!*—the traffic! You'd get out there on the freeway and you might just as well take a nap, eat your lunch, whatever—you weren't going anywhere.

Los Angeles was definitely not your "hometown" kind of place. One day you had a neighbor whom you stopped and said hello to and talked about the family, and when you woke up the next morning, he'd moved out—furniture, family, dog, car, everything. No sign or trace of him.

Lou Irwin, Hollywood theatrical agent, chomped on a cigar stump and shouted into the telephone. "Look, take my word fer-t. The kid's *good!* Yeah? So don't take my word fer-t, hire him anyhow!"

It is difficult for me to sit still when I'm nervous, so I began to pace. Another actor sat in a nearby chair, waiting. He was a handsome, friendly man with fine whittled features. His name was Ted Knight. Lou Irwin was talking about him on the telephone.

"You're from New York!" Ted beamed after I had spoken approximately three words. (My diction!) "So am I. Well, that is, almost. I'm from Terryville, Connecticut."

We talked about life "back East" and about performing. Ted was married and had children. He had been with a radio station in Troy, New York, and then another one in Albany. He had done mostly voice work for children's radio and television shows.

"Are you Welsh, with a name like MacLeod?"

"No. I'm part Chippewa and part Swedish—my real name is Allan See."

"At least you can pronounce it. I was born with the

name Tadeus Wladyslaw Konopka. My mother's the only one who can say it right."

A friendship formed between Ted Knight and me that would span nearly thirty years, until cancer took Ted in 1986. Ted filled me in on what to expect in Hollywood— the best way to work with agents, accountants, managers. He told me it was tough for an actor, but no worse than in New York. Then he asked, "How are you going to live?"

I shrugged and smiled. "Have you been talking with my mother?"

Ted told me how hard he worked on his trick voices, playing animals and doing dialects. He had been a graduate of the Randall School of Drama in Rhode Island, and was a voice on the radio program "Superman."

"You spend four years in school studying the classics and your first job after you graduate is imitating a duck."

Ted told me a story about Lou Irwin, the agent we were waiting for. "If Lou can't get us work, nobody can," he said.

"Lou goes to extremes, bends over backward to gain the attention of a director or a producer on behalf of his clients," Ted explained. "Like the time the director Fred Zinnemann ordered a sandwich from the deli near the studio where he was shooting a picture. Lou was handling an actor named George Tobias. He intercepted the deli's delivery boy, so when Mr. Zinnemann unwrapped his sandwich there was a note with big letters: HIRE GEORGE TOBIAS. SIGNED, LOU IRWIN.

Later I would marvel at the audacity of people who are vying for the big time. But just then I was not so much interested in the big time as I was to simply *work*.

One of my first jobs in Los Angeles was co-starring with Jocelyn Brando (Marlon's sister), Brian Hutton, Robert

("Barretta") Blake, and Al Lettieri in *Hatful of Rain* at the Players Ring Gallery Theatre. Among other roles as a "heavy" was my role in *The Connection*, a play about junkies hanging around waiting for a fix.

I became accustomed to hearing, "You're a fabulous junkie and dope pusher," and I didn't know whether or not to take it as a compliment when I was told, "You make it easy to hate you."

Robert Wise gave me a screen test for the movie *Run Silent, Run Deep*, which starred Clark Gable. Though Robert Wise carefully considered me, I didn't get the part I tested for. (I lost out to another up-and-coming talent by the name of Don Rickles.) But as it often happens in show business, the performance wasn't for nothing. Robert Wise remembered me when casting began for the Susan Hayward movie *I Want to Live* in 1958.

"Oh, how I want the part of the husband-drug addict," I told Ted Knight. Playing addicts seemed to be my specialty. "Gavin," Ted said, "if you play that role in the Susan Hayward picture, people are going to flock to the movie houses just to throw tomatoes at you."

I didn't get the part. Instead, I was cast as a police lieutenant who had one intimidating scene interrogating Susan Hayward, who played a woman sentenced to the gas chamber despite her protests of innocence. At one point, I was to yank her hair. When I told Mom, she wrote me, "Do they *pay* you to act so mean? You were always such a *nice* boy—"

"I'm getting the best education an actor can get on this movie," I told her. I was grateful to Robert Wise for his choice in casting. I admired the director and always will. If I could pick the man I'd want as a father, it would be Robert Wise.

On March 5, 1960, my son Keith was born. He was the bright light in my life. I handed out cigars and promised myself I would never drink like my father. "No sir, I'm going to be there for my son. I'm going to show him life, hand him the world, give him the love I always wanted."

But I didn't keep my word.

Before you could say, "Captain Kangaroo," I was off on tour with a play. After returning to the West Coast, I began smoking heavily and overeating. Slowly but surely, the optimistic, happy-go-lucky guy became loud and often morose.

"It's called *growth*," I tried to explain to Rootie. "You can't stop a man from growing. And I do *not* drink too much. Don't expect me to stay the kid just out of college you met a few years ago. Don't expect me to stay an elevator operator." It wasn't the first of our fights. I was a man "on the way up." And not as an elevator operator.

There I was, in my first major motion picture. And I was working with the great Susan Hayward! In person, she was a tiny little lady, so gracious. She played Barbara Graham, a woman sentenced to the gas chamber. My one big scene interrogating her took a whole day to shoot. A great scene. Susan Hayward threw coffee on me and I screamed and yelled at her, pulled her hair. Oh, we were a dramatic sensation.

So then the movie came out, and I went to see it in a Beverly Hills theatre. I was all excited. There was only one old lady in the theatre besides me. It came time for my scene and my heart was beating fast. I waited. No scene! They cut it so short there was nothing left to it. If you blinked you missed it. I let out a howl, and the old lady snapped, "Quiet!" So that was my big film debut. Robert Wise informed me later that the Los Angeles Police Commission wouldn't allow the interrogation scenes. Too violent. That's show biz for you, right?

I continued playing heavies—a pilot film for director Blake Edwards as the lead heavy in "Gunn" (1958), and a small but nice part in the motion picture *Operation Petticoat* with Cary Grant (1959).

I played small roles in two other movies that year, *Pork*

Chop Hill, a Korean War story with Gregory Peck, Harry Guardino, Rip Torn, and George Peppard, and *Compulsion,* about the trial of two Chicago students, Leopold and Loeb, who kidnapped and murdered a young boy for kicks. It starred Dean Stockwell, Bradford Dillman, and Orson Welles. I never stopped running.

I was clearly nothing at all like the young man who operated the elevator at Radio City Music Hall when Rootie and I met. I was a driven person.

"Why should I be the same as ten years ago?" I'd say. "Stop telling me I'm not the same person I once was! Stop nagging me!" I was drinking more now. At a barbecue at the Knights' house in the Valley, Ted's wife, Dottie, implored me, "Gavin, what are you doing to yourself? Do you want to self-destruct?" She even added, "Please don't drink so much."

But I wouldn't listen to anyone's advice. I was defensive and moody. In order to calm myself down, relax, and enjoy myself, I drank. I thought I was being the same "fun" guy. I liked to joke and didn't mind being teased about losing my hair. It didn't bother me because most people told me I looked distinguished. I claimed that I started balding when using a radiator-cleaning compound to whiten my hair for the Kurt Weill opera *Down in the Valley* in college. Every time I washed the white out of my hair, I noticed more and more fell out. One day I looked in the sink and it was filled with hair. I joked that they told me the whitener was the best thing to use to look older. But I wanted to look older with white hair, not a bald head!

Our second son, David, was born September 30, 1961. He was the second shining light in my life, and again I played the proud father, handing out cigars to all my

friends. That same year I appeared in the film *High Time*
with Bing Crosby and was shooting another war story,
War Hunt, with Robert Redford.

And I kept drinking. When I returned to New York to
play in the Theatre Guild production of *The Captains and
the Kings*, the Broadway theatre was in transition again.
There were few American dramatists of major significance.
It had been two decades since Tennessee Williams, Arthur
Miller, and William Inge appeared on the horizon, and
original plays were being produced Off Broadway on lower
budgets.

There was a new kind of theatre making its imprint:
Theatre of the Absurd. Plays such as Eugene Ionesco's
Rhinoceros, which showed that human beings could be
transformed into anything, including rhinoceroses, if they
submitted to conformity long enough; Harold Pinter's *The
Caretaker*, naturalism carried to absurdity, and his *Birthday
Party* and *The Homecoming*, which presented amoral situations without emotion. These plays of the sixties were
drawing audiences in what Brooks Atkinson called "a gro-
tesque and faithless period of history."

I didn't know how I would fit into this new theatre
form. Off Broadway, Edward Albee's *Zoo Story* opened,
followed by Arthur Kopit's *Oh Dad, Poor Dad, Mamma's
Hung You in the Closet and I'm Feelin' So Sad* (called "an
exercise in banality"). Lavish musicals such as *My Fair
Lady*, *The Sound of Music*, and *Man of La Mancha* were playing to long, successful runs on Broadway. I wasn't likely
to get hired as a singer and dancer at this stage of my
career; I had a reputation as a heavy. I wanted better and
more varied roles—a chance to expand my repertoire and
prove my versatility. So in the fall of 1962 I returned to
Hollywood and signed a contract with Universal to play

Happy Haines in the popular TV military comedy "McHale's Navy." I remained on the show from 1962 to 1964. Starring actors in the series included Ernest Borgnine, Tim Conway, Joe Flynn, and Gary Vinson. "McHale's Navy" had a superb cast, and for the most part we got along very well with one another. The story centered around a lieutenant commander named McHale (Ernest Borgnine) who commanded a World War II PT boat with his crew of comedy characters. This was a steady job with steady income, security, acceptance. All was well, or at least it should have been. There was still a restlessness, a gnawing within me. Inside I was still that child gazing longingly to the other side of the railroad tracks, where he was certain the real world lay.

I was glad to be co-starring in a comedy series because I wanted to shed my image as a heavy. But there was more sitting around on the set than actual work. I had earned early recognition for my role in *The Connection*, which supposedly represented mankind's need for a "fix" or a "connection" to make life at least momentarily bearable. That was how I felt now—in need of something, but I didn't know what. I realized my marriage was going from bad to worse.

Every morning I stopped on the way to the studio to buy a couple of six-packs or a case of beer. It was "for the boys," I told myself. The producers always provided food for the actors to snack on during the day as they waited for their scenes to be rehearsed or shot. Between the eating and the drinking, I gained more weight. My language and behavior became crude. My priorities were the show, drinking, eating, my children, and my marriage, in that order.

In spite of the beautiful home in Granada Hills, a lovely

wife, and fabulous children, I was moody and unhappy. *There's got to be more than this*, I agonized. For some performers, "actor" is their only identity. There is no other significant fact to record about their lives. I didn't want that to happen to me. Yet, what did I have going for me? I felt trapped at home. I didn't have hobbies, and I had little to share with my family.

I wondered, if I prayed, would anyone hear me? I thought maybe it was a matter of changing my image again. Maybe I should try doing musicals. Or maybe I needed to get out and have a little more fun. Sow some wild oats. Get away from responsibility. . . .

I kept working on the stage in Los Angeles in plays like *Middle of the Night* by Paddy Chayefsky, *The Egg, An Evening of the Absurd, Lullaby,* and *The Web and the Rock,* the latter a play adaptation of the novel by Thomas Wolfe. When a reporter asked me about the direction of my career, I told him, "I have no delusions about stardom. I just want to be good at what I do." I never had the opportunity to study at the Neighborhood Playhouse in New York with Sanford Meisner or at the Actors Studio with Lee Strasberg, but I had worked with the best directors and some of the world's finest actors. You might say the work itself was my school.

I was pleased to earn a reputation in professional circles in Hollywood and New York as a good and versatile actor. I was responsible, prompt; I learned my lines; I was easy to get along with and didn't have a star complex. Although I wasn't well known to audiences, directors and producers knew me and liked my work. I could make a role my own, and I was told this is one factor in distinguishing a good actor from a mediocre one. I played a broad range of parts, from tough soldiers in war to situation-comedy funnymen, like the jewelry salesman in the segment called "Carlotta's Necklace" on "The Dick Van Dyke Show" in 1961. Mary Tyler Moore co-starred in that series.

I was scheduled to play a delicatessen owner with a crush on Rose Marie in a later "Dick Van Dyke" episode, but unfortunately that performance was one of the few in my life I was unable to do because of illness. On Sunday of that Memorial Day weekend, I became so sick with stomach pains I had to be rushed to Holy Cross Hospital in Granada Hills. The physician in the emergency room thought I had a ruptured appendix and told me to cancel work the next day.

"I can't do that," I argued. "We're shooting the show tomorrow. I *must* be at the studio."

The doctor was just as insistent. "You aren't leaving this hospital. You are a very sick man."

"But it's too late to get a replacement for me!" The pain was so intense, I finally stopped arguing and called Carl Reiner to find a replacement for me. I remained in the hospital four days, but it wasn't my appendix after all. It was colitis. I told the doctor, "You should have taken my appendix out just to make it look good. It's like going to the movies and there's nothing playing."

In the sixties, I played a small part in a movie called *The Brink's Robbery*, starring Peter Falk and Peter Boyle. It was about the famous Boston heist of 1950. I played the guy who drives the truck. When it was time to shoot my first scene, I climbed into the truck, just as rehearsed, and—we went nowhere. Nobody had said anything about a stick shift! The actor in the other truck couldn't drive a stick shift either, so we all sat there. The famous moment in crime history went absolutely nowhere. It was so funny, it's too bad we couldn't have rewritten the script and left it in.

In January 1964, our first daughter, Julie, was born. We were thrilled. I celebrated by drinking.

But I worked even harder now. I played in *Twelve Hours to Kill* with Barbara Eden and *The Sword of Ali Baba* (1965). On television (fast becoming my best medium) I appeared on the police drama "The Untouchables," starring Robert Stack, several times during its 1961–1963 run. Occasionally I had a chance to play comedy, such as Pamela Britton's younger brother in "My Favorite Martian," the comedy series which ran from 1963 to 1966.

I played in the 1965–1968 series "Run for Your Life," starring Ben Gazzara, and also "Hogan's Heroes," the comedy series set in a Nazi POW camp during World War II. I was starting to feel secure.

To the folks back in Pleasantville, I was a big Hollywood actor, a celebrity. Mom saved the clippings I sent and passed them around to her family and co-workers at the bank.

My brother, Ron, hadn't found it easy to follow in my footsteps. Even though the love between us was deep and strong, he felt he was in the shadow of his big Hollywood actor brother. Ever since we were little boys I had watched over Ronnie, loved him, protected him, and been his friend. But now people met him on the street with, "So, Ron, what do you hear from Allan? What movie is he shooting now?" Or, "Does your brother *really* know Robert Redford?" Or, "Can your brother get me a job in the movies?" Or, even worse, "How come you're not like your brother? He's *so* talented." I never thought of myself as handsome, so when Ron told me the girls were clamoring to meet me, we got a big laugh out of it. "It's all done with lights," I said.

Once when we sat talking late into the night, Ron said to me, "Do you ever think about Dad? I mean, his dying . . . ?"

"You mean his dying at thirty-nine?"

"Yeah . . . do you ever wonder if maybe you won't make it past thirty-nine?"

I felt an odd sense of relief. He had put into words something I had always tried not to face. It was as if I had been frantically trying to achieve all I could before the inevitable doom. "You remember how Dad dreaded hitting thirty-nine? He just knew that was his year to go. . . ."

"And he knew he'd die of cancer. . . ."

"Because of Vet Fowler."

We were quiet. It was frightening, ominous. Ronnie didn't hide his fears in booze. But I really didn't know what else to do. Now I had to face a new movement in the theatre and find my place in the decade that believed thirty years old was over the hill.

The 1960s was a highly self-conscious decade in America. By the middle of the sixties young people on college campuses were in open revolt against "the system." Years later I read a book on secular humanism by James Hitchcock, a professor of History at St. Louis University. According to Hitchcock, these years were marked by man's dependence upon his own ingenuity. Religion was merely a courtesy occasionally extended to God, "much in the way that one might take time out from a busy schedule to visit an elderly grandparent." That's the way it was for me.

When John Kennedy was assassinated in 1963, the idealism he inspired seemed to die with him. His successor, Lyndon Johnson, carried on his programs with greater success than Kennedy himself, but people were disappointed and realized that poverty and injustice were not going to be eradicated in America. And the Vietnam War loomed real and ugly before all of us. Young people submerged themselves in youth ghettos like the Haight-Ashbury district in San Francisco and the East Village in New York City, where they listened to Timothy Leary preach about the virtues of LSD and endeavored to discover the merits of the "inner self." And a lot of us older people were inspired by the youth protests and rebellion. We wanted to experience "liberation," too.

During that period I felt more and more alienated from Rootie. Our fourth baby was born in 1965, a beautiful little girl we named Meghan. I was now the father of *four* wonderful, loving, sweet kids. I loved them so much, yet I dug into work with a zeal that kept me from taking time off or going on family vacations. When director Robert Wise offered me a role in the movie *The Sand Pebbles*, I jumped at it. It meant going on location to the Far East. I was excited about working with Robert Wise again, and I liked the script and the stars who were in the film. The story was about an American gunboat patrolling the Yangtze River in 1926 and its involvement with Chinese warlords. Its stars were Steve McQueen, Candice Bergen, Richard Attenborough, and Richard Crenna. It would earn an Academy Award nomination for the best movie of the year.

I was thirty-four years old, still finding myself. Would I ever land leading roles in films or on TV? Would I ever get recognition for my work? Would I ever receive an Emmy or a Tony or an Oscar? I was worried about not being taken seriously in my profession. I knew actors who were content to play small parts all their lives. I knew the adage, "There are no small parts—only small actors," and for the most part I felt grateful just to be working, to be able to put food on the table and pay the bills. But I was also chang-

ing, becoming more and more restless, and the old gnawing, unfulfilled feelings remained in me.

I left for Taiwan to shoot *The Sand Pebbles*, hoping it
would take my mind off things at home and the problems
between Rootie and me. I was drinking heavily and gaining more weight, but it didn't bother me. I didn't think
about the effect drinking might have on my work.

It didn't occur to me that taking off for a six-month trip,
leaving a wife and four small children behind, was wrong.
I thought of my wife as capable, cold, and efficient. But the
children—my heart warmed when I thought of them. They
were loving toward me, always happy to see me, undemanding, eager to please. My drinking had not yet de-
moralized them. I hadn't insulted them in public, lied,
cheated, or taken my rage out on them. I was blind to the
situation. I thought of the family much the same way my
father and his father's father thought of a family. They
were a unit unto themselves with an efficient woman at
the helm. I was their financier, and I felt that I deserved
more attention and love than I got. If I had been more
open to the God of love and kindness, I might have seen
how desperately my family needed, loved, and wanted
me to be a part of them.

But I told myself everything was all right: *Just keep laughing and thinking positively, Gavin, old boy. That's show biz,
right?*

Working on *The Sand Pebbles* wasn't what I expected. I
thought I'd be traveling and working with the large cast
and crew, but I was sent ahead; I was the cover scene in
case of rain. That meant traveling from Los Angeles to
Hawaii alone, from Hawaii to Guam alone; then to Tokyo
and Taiwan and Taipei alone.

In Taipei I had a few moments alone with Steve

McQueen. We were standing outside our hotel in a torrent of rain and Steve grabbed my arm and said, "Hiya brother!" because we had played brothers in *Hatful of Rain* in New York almost ten years earlier.

"Gav, did you ever think we'd wind up here in the Orient in a motion picture?"

"You're getting drenched in the rain, Steve," I said.

"Did you ever think I'd get where I am today?"

"You've done great for yourself, Steve," I answered.

"Right, brother. I've done pretty good for a grease monkey from the West Side, huh?" (In the early fifties, he had worked as a mechanic in a garage on West Sixty-ninth Street in New York City.)

"You've done great, Steve. What's happened to you and your career is terrific."

"A lot of people said I'd never make it."

"Yeah, well, they were all wrong."

We moved from beneath the awning outside the hotel toward the lobby inside. The rain continued to hammer downward. It was the last serious talk I ever had with Steve McQueen. It was like that old joke, ". . . but let me stop talking about myself. What do *you* think about me?"

In the long, late nights I did get to thinking—in time the work runs out, and if your entire identity comes through your work, what happens when the work isn't there anymore? What's real about an actor? What's real about life? Is there a God who is real?

When I talked like that, Candy Bergen told me I was being too serious. After all, life is to be enjoyed.

"I agree! I've always believed that," I answered. "But what happens when you wake up one day and realize you really are *nothing?*"

You start drinking, I thought. *Or you take drugs.* Like some of the old stars, the so-called has-beens who can't cope with *not* being a star anymore.

Between the beer and the heat of the Taiwan air, I was sluggish and morose. Besides, I had gained so much weight that the crew and cast were calling me Moby Dick.

I wrote long letters home, making promises to Rootie never to leave again, to become a real family man, but they were promises I couldn't keep. When I got back to California I drank even more heavily; I started taking pills to lose weight and I became elusive, internalizing my feelings, not communicating. I still had little time for the family.

In despair one night I tried to take my own life. The attempt was a failure and I wasn't sure which depressed me more—the fact that I had tried to commit suicide or that I couldn't.

My reaction was typical: more work. I began training for musical comedy. I had a dream of a Broadway musical comedy starring *me*.

I now screamed at Rootie in public. I left her at parties to get home by herself; I ranted and howled at home so that the children became frightened and intimidated. Many mornings when I woke up in my own bed, I was unsure how I got there. I began blacking out more and more, and losing control.

Even with these warnings, at work I still portrayed the jovial, positive, fun-loving guy. One day in the makeup room I sat staring at the veiled, distant eyes in the mirror. They were the same eyes of my father and his father before him—clouded, far off, as though protecting us from the knowledge of what we did.

The seventies were good years for war movies. *Patton* won the Oscar for best movie of the year in 1970. I was in another war movie for MGM, *Kelly's Heroes,* starring Clint Eastwood. I felt doomed to play soldiers in war movies forever. This one was about an American platoon that discovered a fortune in gold. It was partially filmed in Yugoslavia. So again I was a stranger to my family.

I auditioned for the lead in the Rodgers and Hammerstein World War II musical comedy, *Carousel,* and landed the part of Jigger. It was an opportunity to show a side of me that audiences were not yet familiar with. The role required singing as well as dramatic acting. During rehearsals, my agent called and told me about the Lou Grant role in a new television series for CBS, "The Mary Tyler Moore Show." The producers sent me a script and after reading it over I went in for my first interview with the writers, James Brooks and Alan Burns, and the casting director, Ethel Wynant. I read the part of Lou Grant. They thanked me and as I was leaving I turned and said, "I really like the part of Murray. Do you think I could read Murray for you?"

Alan Burns said, "But that isn't a part for an actor like you. I don't know if you would like playing such a laid-back, nonemotional role."

"I think I'd love it. I may never become the 'Marcello Mastroianni of Minneapolis' [a Murray description of Ted Baxter] but I think I would really like to play Murray."

I read for the part, and on my way out I passed Ed Asner, who was on his way in to audition for Lou Grant. He looked confident, serious. There's nothing more irritating than a talented actor who is reading for a part you're up for and he's *confident*. I was overjoyed when Ed got the part of Lou Grant because I knew then that Murray was mine.

The most difficult part to cast was that of Ted Baxter because the producers wanted a young actor who could be funny and romantic—someone like Jack Cassidy. But Ted Knight was perfect. I always believed Ted was one of the best actors in Hollywood, and he proved it when he read for the role of the narcissistic newscaster. Sheer comedic genius.

I was in rehearsal for *Carousel* when my agent called and told me I had the part of Murray. I was excited about it because I felt it was the start of something wonderful in my career. Besides, I'd be working with such talented people, including my old buddy Ted. A lot of actors auditioned for the show and one actor who didn't make it grumbled that getting hired in a show was just a matter of good luck. I loved Ted's answer. He said, "It's hard for me to recognize good luck. It looks too much like something we've earned."

Ted and I went out to celebrate and talked about the show.

"Ted, you've played heavies for most of your career. Now you're playing one of the funniest characters I've ever seen in my life. You are hilarious. You just put me away."

"You and I have both played a lot of heavies, haven't

we, Gavin? I've played statesmen, politicians, Shake-speare, you name it."

"This is an incredible switch for us," I said. Ted Baxter was a far cry from Ted's role as the H.L. Mencken character in *Inherit the Wind*. And my role of newswriter Murray Slaughter, everybody's-big-brother-and-friend type of guy, was hardly my junkie character in *The Connection*. Murray was supportive, tenderhearted, and funny, but not showy. Ted and I would have many conversations about our roles.

"You're too nice—too modest, Gavin," he'd tell me.

"I need three press agents to tell the world how modest I am," I said. I stayed with the show from the day it went on the air in 1970 until the last taping in February 1977, appearing in every episode. "The Mary Tyler Moore Show" made television history. Throughout its seven-year run, the cast was like a family. Ted and Ed Asner were like brothers to me, and Mary was the mother of us all. Mary was always conscious of diet and staying in shape. A big thrill for Mary and Valerie Harper was opening the cookie jar on the set and just *smelling*.

The show generated stars and other series. Cloris Leachman played Phyllis Lindstrom from 1970 until 1975 and then left for her own series, "Phyllis." Valerie Harper was with the show from 1970 until 1974, when she left for her own series, "Rhoda." Betty White and Georgia Engel completed the close family of actors. The show became the keystone of the colorful CBS Saturday-night lineup, and after seven happy years it went off the air at the height of its popularity. A *Ladies' Home Journal* poll taken among high school students in 1976 showed that high school boys rated Mary Tyler Moore number ten on their list of top heroines of the year, and the girls voted her number six.

On the first day of rehearsals, Ed and I talked about the time we were both up for a part in *In the Heat of the Night* back in 1967 in New York. That part had called for a fat, slovenly guy, and the producers called Ed and me to read for it. We laughed about it now because the director, Norman Jewison, hired skinny Warren Oates for the role.

Ed and I had been around a long time. He played Mr. Peecham in *Three Penny Opera* with Bea Arthur in New York, did Shakespeare in the Park, and was with the Compass Players in Chicago.

The cast was made up of skilled actors who brought incredible joy to their characters. Cloris Leachman was a stunning actress. She later won an Academy Award for her role in *The Last Picture Show*. Valerie Harper and I became special friends, especially during our weight-loss periods. Every time Valerie went on a diet, so did I. It was a riot because we weighed every crumb we ate—we counted every calorie. She thought I was a nice guy and I loved her like the little sister I never had. We laughed like kids, and that's because Valerie is the kind of person who makes everything funny. She teased me about my love for food. "There's something very Italian in that little Chippewa heart of yours," she'd tell me.

In the early seventies with MTM, my career took off. I finally felt secure in the direction I was heading. I was playing in Rodgers and Hammerstein's *Carousel* at night and rehearsing during the day for "The Mary Tyler Moore Show." My role in *Carousel* was a complicated and difficult one. The best thing about the show was that my children were with me. They played the Snow children. It was a special time for us, driving to the theatre together, working together, and being together. Driving home after the show, they always fell asleep, and I looked at their little faces and thought of the words of Billy Bigalow's intimate soliloquy toward the end of act 1, a piece speculating on what his child might be like.

I often brought my children to the Friday-night tapings of "The Mary Tyler Moore Show." Julie, who was seven years old in 1970 at the start of the series, told all her friends, "My daddy works on 'The Tiny Miley Moore Show.' "

Valerie loved it. She immediately adapted the name for Mary and listed her phone number as "Tiny Miley."

But life at home was difficult despite my resolve to be a better father. In 1972 I became involved with a theatre group called Words and Music. Aspiring actors and actresses as well as the stars studied acting and musical theatre and then performed productions in a converted garage with only ninety-nine seats. The garage was called the Words and Music Theatre, located in Van Nuys. It was a showcase for stars such as Loretta Swit, John Anderson, and Jed Allen to do special projects.

In 1971 the group produced *The Chocolate Soldier*, a revival of the 1947 Oskar Straus musical. It was a silly little play and I thoroughly enjoyed it.

> Come! Come! I love you o-o-only
> My heart is tru-u-u-u-e.

Great stuff. I thought the best thing in the production was the cute little dancer with the long, blond braids, Patti Steele. After the performance I told her backstage I enjoyed her in the show and she, in turn, told me she enjoyed me on "The Mary Tyler Moore Show," and that her daughter, Stephanie, was in a series right before mine on the same network. (Stephanie co-starred in a situation comedy called "Arnie," starring Herschel Bernardi.)

I started taking tap dancing in a class taught by Patti. She thought I was funny, even though I often disrupted her class. "Do you think I'll ever be a tap dancer like Fred Astaire?" I asked Patti after class one day. She looked at me and sighed.

"More like Attila the Hun."

The next show Words and Music produced was *A Funny Thing Happened on the Way to the Forum*. I starred as Pseudolus. Patti played one of the Gemini Twins. It was a ribald comedy, and I frolicked and cavorted my way through it to praise reviews.

We followed with the musical *High Button Shoes*. I starred and Patti choreographed it. Now we were becoming good friends. Patti was concerned for my health because I was almost one hundred pounds overweight and she saw that my drinking habits were serious. Patti knew a lot about diet and nutrition because she had so many allergies and was always on a new health regimen.

We were now talking to each other every day on the telephone. Patti was worried about my mental attitude. "Gavin, you're like a Wagnerian opera hidden behind a Gilbert and Sullivan front," she said.

I became especially inconsolable when the Emmys were presented one year and everyone on "The Mary Tyler Moore Show" was nominated except me.

I had promised Patti to help her find an agent. She telephoned one day to make arrangements for an interview. Meghan, my youngest daughter, answered the phone and said, "My dad can't talk to you—he's sick."

"But I heard your dad never gets sick."

". . . well, he's . . . sick now."

I was hiding—utterly crushed over the Emmy nominations—and I had gotten drunk.

Every year the National Academy of Television Arts and Sciences presents the Emmy Awards to recognize excellence in television performance and production. The Emmys are to the television industry what the Academy Awards are to the motion picture industry. Naturally, every performer on television would like to be recognized with an Emmy. The Emmy Awards for the 1971–72 television season were presented on May 6, 1972, and for its first year on the air, "The Mary Tyler Moore Show" won two awards for Outstanding Performances by Valerie Harper and Ed Asner. Naturally, I was happy for the winners and congratulated them.

The Emmys for the 1972–73 season were presented May 22, 1973, and "The Mary Tyler Moore Show" received four of the awards. Director Jay Sandrich was recognized for Outstanding Directorial Achievement, and the actors who won Outstanding Performance awards were Mary Tyler Moore, Ted Knight, and Valerie Harper. I tried to hide my disappointment.

The following year, on May 28, the awards for the 1973–74 season were announced. Again the show took four awards, two of them going to Mary as Best Actress and Actress of the Year, another to Cloris Leachman, and one to Treva Silverman as Writer of the Year for a series. It was getting more difficult to smile each year.

The biggest year for the show was the 1974–75 season, when "The Mary Tyler Moore Show" swept away eight of the Emmys, including Outstanding Comedy Series of the Year and Outstanding Writing, with Outstanding Performance awards going to Ted Knight, Betty White, Cloris Leachman, Ed Asner, and Valerie Harper. By now, I dreaded the Emmy Awards.

Again in 1976 on May 17, when the 1975–76 awards

were presented, "The Mary Tyler Moore Show" won more Emmys than any other series, including Outstanding Comedy Series. Mary was again Outstanding Lead Actress, David Lloyd won an Outstanding Writing Award, and Ted Knight and Betty White earned Outstanding Performance awards. I was utterly crushed to be left out again.

The last year the show aired, the Emmys were presented on September 12, 1977, for the 1976–77 season. Once more "The Mary Tyler Moore Show" won Outstanding Comedy Series, and the final episode of the show won an Emmy for Outstanding Writing.

There was one name consistently missing from the list of Emmy Awards, and that person was inconsolable. I played the amiable Murray with as much heart as I could muster. In one episode Murray's dreams are dashed when he discovers he'll always be a hack writer. He laments to Mary, "I just have to face it, Mair, I'll never be a literary giant writing copy for the six o'clock news."

When I spoke those lines, I didn't know who to feel sorrier for—Murray or myself.

I rented a little place on the beach in Oxnard and called it Camelot by the Sea. I realized that eight years of marriage therapy only proved my marriage was beyond repair. In the past I had tried to end it several times, and during my many drinking sprees I had gotten temporarily involved in other relationships, moved out, moved back home, thrown fits—now it was over.

Patti and I were both lonely and looking for love. Together we laughed a lot and it felt good. We worked in the musicals, listened to records, went for walks, and did a lot of talking. We were both forty-one years old, neither one of us wanting to admit we were growing older. The inevitable happened. We fell in love.

We began openly dating, but it wasn't until after my divorce in 1973 that we made plans for our wedding.

It was so hard to tell my kids about the divorce. I took them out to the backyard to tell them their mother and I were getting a divorce. David kicked the Ping-Pong table. First the dog had died, he said, and now this. "There's nothing around here that I like," he cried. I felt horrible. And my girls just cried—so did I.

The next week, when I went over to the house to pick up a few of my things, I heard the children outside. They weren't laughing and playing as usual. They had a little lemonade stand set up and the neighborhood kids were there and Meghan was telling them, "My daddy's getting a bivorce." Keith, the oldest, was sullen. David didn't talk and Julie cried. We all cried. They wanted to hate me and their suffering upset me more than anything.

But what hurts me more is to think of them crying in their beds while I was drunk and raving like a madman in the other room with their mother. I hurt them and her, as well as everyone dear to me—and no matter what I do now, I can't take those years back.

Patti and I were married on February 22, George Washington's birthday, in 1974. We thought it was appropriate because we both liked George Washington. We laughed, calling him the country's first stand-up comic with lines like, "I'm not sure I'd have crossed the Delaware if I had known New Jersey was on the other side." By marrying Patti I hoped for a happier, fun life with laughter ringing around us and no hassles. I went into the marriage with both feet planted squarely in the clouds.

Patti knew I hated to deal with anything negative. She wanted me to open up and talk to her. She wanted me to *talk* all the time. But to me it wasn't talking, it was like *digging*—it was *probing.* I just wanted to be happy. I thought getting a divorce from Rootie would make me happy. If things weren't happy, I didn't want to think or know about it. Drinking was a part of all that. But Patti and I had such great moments working together. Most of the time it was terrific. I just wanted to laugh, be happy, have fun.

In 1973, before Patti and I were married, I did *Gypsy* with Kay Ballard in San Diego. I played Herbie, the boyfriend of Mama Rose. Kay was a riot. But I didn't feel well. Kay said I was terrific, of course, but I felt my health slipping.

During "The Mary Tyler Moore Show" I kept gaining weight. I wore a black sweater so often on the show that people in the cast started to joke about it. One day Ted saw me sitting on the set, wearing the black sweater as usual, and said, "Now I get it! There's a mask in your pocket and all this time you've been down the hall doubling as Zorro. Right?"

Ted took such good care of himself. He and Dottie ate healthy food, exercised, played tennis. Ted was into fitness. And of course, so was Mary. She never deviated from her strict diet, she exercised, held regular noon-hour ballet classes on the set, which Patti attended, and held herself with that perfect, erect posture at all times. She was perfectly disciplined in every way. But me? I guess I thought I was disciplined. I was a totally punctual person, I was never late (for work, that is), I learned my lines, I worked hard—all those things. But the weight problem got out of hand. And so did the drinking. It was the hardest thing in the world for me to admit I was an alcoholic. Patti was the one who eventually made me face it because I tried to hide it from the rest of the world.

I finally realized that for an alcoholic, denial serves as a kind of functional blindness. It keeps the drinker in a state of unawareness. The alcoholic rationalizes and defends himself against profound insecurity and low self-esteem. The alcoholic does not say, "I drink because I have no control over alcohol." He says, "I drink because my wife doesn't understand me," or "I drink because of life's pressures," or "I drink when I feel depressed."

My drinking was out of control, and it led to other health problems. I suffered from gout; my body was bloated; I was often in pain and tired. My abdomen was distended so badly that the swelling pressed on my lungs and impaired my breathing. Once I became so ill, feverish and vomiting, that my skin looked green. I was admitted to the hospital in Granada Hills and diagnosed as having ileitis, which is a serious disorder of the intestines. And I had colitis.

When Patti read the diet that the hospital dietician had given me, she said, "Let's rip that thing up, Gavin. You want to get well? I'll help you get well. But you'll have to trust me." Because of her allergies, she had been living on strange diets all her life. She was a real nutrition junkie.

But I trusted her. In late 1973 we drove from Los Angeles down to the desert community of Escondido, just east of San Diego, to a naturopath. After a careful examination and lengthy interview, the doctor told me, "If you take one more cigarette or one more drink of alcohol, including beer or wine, you could die." He prescribed a total change in diet including distilled water and herb-, vitamin-, and mineral-supplement therapy.

He told me about the scientific discoveries showing that alcoholism may be due to an inherited metabolic defect. In other words, it isn't always due to some character defect or personal weakness. Some people can drink moderately, others cannot. If this is the case, he said, the right nutrients are necessary to change and stabilize the body's biochemistry. He explained that the average person makes about one ounce of alcohol every day by normal metabolism, and in order to metabolize this alcohol, special enzymes in the liver convert alcohol to a chemical which, when overloading the system, can damage the body. Adding extra alcohol to the body, then, creates abnormal chemical bonds in proteins, causing abnormal cell function. I didn't know that alcoholics have a metabolic defect that results in their having twice the amount of harmful chemicals in their bloodstream as normal people after taking a drink. The alcohol itself is actually less harmful than the chemical it creates because the body can't get rid of it easily. I realized I could never drink again, not only for behavioral reasons but also because my body couldn't handle it.

First the doctor said I had to detoxify with a week-long fast. Patti tucked me in bed and nursed me with a detoxifying fast of distilled water for one week. (I had been drinking a six-pack of beer at breakfast at the time.) I began working on getting healthy. It took time, but slowly my health improved. I lost seventy pounds, quit smoking, ate no red meat, and maintained the strict diet the naturopath prescribed. I faithfully downed my mountain of vitamin and mineral supplements six times a day. Ed Asner commented on how good I was looking and I joked, "Well, I won't have to borrow your clothes any longer, Ed."

The show was another anchor of stability for me—a working family. There would be guests, mostly our families, on the sets at rehearsals and the tapings on Friday nights. Mary's sister, Liz, was usually there, and Mary's son, Richie. Ted's kids would be there, Ed's kids, mine, and Patti's.

I loved Richie, Mary's son. He was someone really special. One of the reasons we struck up such a good friendship was that he played the drums, and I used to play the drums when I was a kid. He told me his neighbors complained when he practiced. My advice was, "Until you smell smoke, ignore it." He thought that was pretty funny.

When Richie was accidentally killed in 1980 at the age of nineteen, we hurt with Mary, but that's all we could do. When I look back on it now, I see that a lot of the hurt and fear in my own life in those days was because of no real sense of eternal security. I put everything I had into my work, but I knew deep down it wasn't enough. I came up short as a person.

When "The Mary Tyler Moore Show" ended in 1977, I had four offers for other shows. I read the scripts and was unimpressed. I told Patti, "You'd think we lived in a world populated entirely with detectives, gangsters, thugs, cops, doctors, and sick people."

She stared at me blankly. "You mean we don't?"

My agent sent me a pilot script called "The Love Boat," and I thought he was kidding about that title. I read it in Palm Springs while Patti and I were busy packing and moving. I liked it. Patti liked it. The pool man liked it. Patti said it was about time I had a starring role because I was always the star in her eyes. I was hysterical at the idea of something called "The Love Boat," but I really liked the role of the Captain. The show seemed like an ideal mix of comedy, love story, and a serious story, all happening simultaneously. At that time it was unique.

We got back to Los Angeles and were trying to figure out which pieces of furniture we could fit into our little studio apartment in Santa Monica, when I received a call to meet with Aaron Spelling at his estate in Beverly Hills to talk about "The Love Boat." When I arrived, all the major people were there: Aaron, Doug Cramer, the executive producer, and Henry Colman, line producer.

Later Aaron told me, "I wasn't sure if you were all that interested. But the more we talked, the more excited you became about the show. I saw you generating excitement, and when the meeting was over, I called ABC and said, 'We have to have Gavin MacLeod. He's perfect.' "

Henry Colman announced to the news media: "Gavin's warmth was the catalyst we needed—we wanted heart, not a ramrod captain . . . and Gavin was all that and more."

I had lost weight with Patti's influence and unflagging help. My skin was tanned by Palm Spring's blessed sun and my eyes were bright and clear of the alcoholic haze. I felt great. The problems with my colon had all but disappeared with the naturopath's nutritional plan and Patti's implementing every detail. She was determined to make me well and to be the best wife in the whole world.

Meanwhile, I was signed to play Charlie Davenport in *Annie Get Your Gun*, which would open in June in San Francisco. I learned the part for *Annie* while shooting the pilot for "The Love Boat." Then it was a matter of waiting to see whether or not ABC would pick up the show. Just before opening in San Francisco, Aaron called and told me the show had been sold to ABC. I worked out an arrangement where I performed in *Annie Get Your Gun* in San Francisco at night, flew back to Los Angeles on the red-eye flight, arrived home at 2:00 A.M., shot "The Love Boat" all the following day, and flew back in time to go on again in *Annie Get Your Gun* at night. It was insanity and I loved it.

Patti told friends, "There's a man who falls into my bed about two-thirty every morning and leaves at six. I just hope to goodness it's my husband!"

"The Love Boat" was touted as TV's first floating singles bar. But it still fell under the "family entertainment" category because there was no violence or bad language. It took place on a luxury cruise liner, the *Pacific Princess*, which each week embarked on a voyage of comic skits, all dealing with love and featuring Hollywood's most durable names, including Carol Channing, Raymond Burr, Ethel Merman, Lana Turner, June Allyson, Jane Wyman, Ruth Gordon, Pearl Bailey, Ray Bolger, Maurice Evans, and countless others.

When "The Love Boat" was aired in the 1977–78 season, the critics had a field day panning it. The show was torpedoed up one side and down the other. It was called the "mothball fleet" because many of the guest stars were older film stars, and it was predicted the show would "sink like the *Titanic*." *Newsweek* hit hard: "The captain of this cruise ship of fools is a prissy curmudgeon who would rather have his fingernails extracted than be nice to his crew."

When Shakespeare said, "All the world's a stage," he forgot to mention the critics. I was undaunted by bad reviews. I believed from the beginning that we would be a hit. At first my character was hard and tough. I remember playing scenes standing on the deck with the collar of a black coat pulled up, the wind blowing, and I'd be snarling and showing my teeth like Kirk Douglas. I was more like Captain Hook than the captain of a vacation cruise ship. I convinced the producers to let me play the Captain with more sensitivity, and it paid off.

Aaron Spelling later told the press, "At first the role of the Captain was so straight and staunch and true to the sea that he wasn't any fun. Gavin gave the role the credibility of a man who could run his ship and also be a person with stories of his own. I think that's what made the show work. Gavin could do anything. He could do heartbreaking love stories; he could do comedies and very touching stories with his TV daughter. Then there was the segment about the loss of his wife."

The bottom line is, what do people want to see? I think that's what television is all about: meeting people where they're at. You can approach TV intellectually, artistically, and come up with a show that dies. You could rip to shreds a light, fun show by making it something people don't want to see. Television is a commercial medium and people will watch what they want to watch.

One hundred million people chose "The Love Boat" every Saturday night. I think one of the reasons people were so supportive of me personally was that they saw me as Murray who, for all those years, got no recognition. Now it was as if Murray had finally made it. He was no longer last banana in a newsroom. He was a *captain*.

Throughout the late seventies and early eighties, Patti and I worked a lot together. In fact, just two months after our wedding in 1974, we went out on tour in the George Axelrod comedy *Seven Year Itch*. We were always busy. Between moving and working there was little time left for pleasure. We took part in the *Salute to Bob Hope* benefit. In fact, we began appearing in as many benefits as our schedule would allow. In April 1980 we were hosts on the cerebral palsy "Weekend With the Stars" telethon, and in June we hosted a benefit for the Los Angeles Easter Seal Society. I appeared at benefits for arthritis, a children's home, a Los Angeles Mission, and the American Cancer Society.

In February 1980, CBS aired the miniseries *Scruples*. I played the role of Curt Avery. In May and June, the ABC TV movie *Murder Can Hurt You* aired. I had a ball doing that. I played a lollipop-chewing takeoff on Kojak named NoJack. The movie also starred John Byner, Tony Danza,

Jamie Farr, and Connie Stevens. I shaved my head for the role and told reporters, "It's so easy to take care of." The role was such a departure for me, people didn't even recognize me.

In the August 29, 1980, issue of *Entertainment Today*, Abe Greenberg wrote that I was now "the most visible star on television." With appearances on reruns of "The Love Boat" and "The Mary Tyler Moore Show," plus my other appearances on variety and dramatic specials and movies, I appeared on no less than thirteen hours of show time each week. And I was being seen in ninety-five countries around the world every week.

"The Love Boat" cast had what co-producer Art Baer said was "chemistry" because the five stars on the show clicked immediately. He said Bernie Kopell, Ted Lange, Fred Grandy, Lauren Tewes, and I were electric the first time we were put together.

More than anything, a successful series depends upon casting. Not only did the actors click on camera, we genuinely liked one another off camera. I learned a lot from Mary Tyler Moore about keeping up the morale on a show. As a result, there was always more joking going on, even among the extras and stand-ins, than complaining. Irritability was at a minimum on Sound Stage 10.

I've never been a competitive person. I'm bad at games. I just don't like to compete. So on the series my main concern was for the show, not for how big my role was or how many lines I had each week.

During "The Love Boat" I took time off to do a couple of shows with Marie Osmond when she landed her own variety series. I did the first show of the series in December 1980. We did a sketch together in which she played a very sad little girl. I held her in my arms and sang, "Smile, though your heart is breaking. . . ." It was like singing to one of my own daughters.

Our seventh anniversary, February 22, 1981, was a romantic one, complete with flowers, soft music, and dinner at Chasen's. Patti and I had moved into a larger three-bedroom condominium overlooking the ocean in Santa Monica, and with most of our furniture and art collections still in storage, I felt the condominium would suit us until we found that "perfect" house. I was now one of the highest-paid actors on television, and we could afford to pay top dollar for the condominium in spite of Patti's better judgment.

"The Love Boat" not only increased my salary but also the popularity of cruise vacations to 100 percent occupancy on the two Princess ships, the *Pacific Princess* and the *Island Princess*. People taking a cruise on these ships served as background for the show in location segments. Passengers rarely minded the camera crews and equipment as they spent their vacation as "extras" for the show.

I felt as if we were on top of the world. But it didn't last.

In February Patti gave me a huge fiftieth-birthday party in California, so I threw one for her fiftieth in March at Ted Hook's Backstage Restaurant in New York. I wanted it to be something special for Patti. She told the fifty guests that things had definitely improved since our wedding, when I had given her a puppy. In reality, I think what she wanted most was more time with me.

The events of 1981 are hazily sketched in my mind. It was the year that seemed to start out so perfectly, and then in a profusion of dust and smoke, exploded in a million pieces.

In April the *National Enquirer* ran an article on how "The Love Boat" cast had been squabbling over getting better lines and bigger parts. These articles usually used expressions like, "According to insiders" and "One source has said" and "A behind-the-scenes person adds. . . ." I was credited as being the peacemaker in all skirmishes and was purported to be giving speeches to convince the cast members to appreciate all the blessings the show had brought them.

Actually, the cast was extremely professional and got along quite well, considering none of us were playing really showy roles. At times I got a bit tired of *smiling*. I would have liked a bit more challenge in acting, but drama and passion simply weren't in the Captain's character. Even when he fell in love with Marion Ross and there was a big wedding episode, he wasn't a Barrymore or Valentino. He was fatherly, smiling Captain Merrill Stubing—in love. Aaron Spelling always called me "the quarterback" of the show. "Gavin, a show's success revolves around its quarterback. You're the one who keeps the sanity on the sound stage. You're like having a multiple offense, if you don't mind my sounding corny.''

Mind? I loved it.

In May, ''The Love Boat'' set sail for the Fiji Islands and Australia, where the fifth-season premiere was to be filmed. In one scene on the two-hour episode, I was to walk cruise director Julie, played by Lauren Tewes, down the aisle for her marriage to an Australian veterinarian. The scene was shot at a beautiful early-nineteenth-century church in Sydney. On the last day of the shooting, standing outside the church, I tripped on the cobblestone and fell, hitting my head on a camera. I was carried off the set where a doctor examined me, and though my head wasn't seriously hurt, my left ankle was broken.

Henry Colman, co-producer of the show, rushed me to the hospital. My foot and ankle were set in a plaster cast and the final shot was made. They put me on a dolly and pulled it so it looked as if I were walking up the aisle. The cameras shot me from the waist up.

In spite of the mishap, we enjoyed the trip. But underneath it all, dissatisfaction was brewing within me. More and more, I felt I needed some changes in my life.

I loved Patti from the time we first met. In the beginning I thought she was funny, alive. But then I started to feel her becoming "bossy." I felt as if she were trying to dominate my life. Sometimes she'd get me in a corner and really let me have it about how I didn't talk to her or care. One time she started in front of my secretary and I said, "Cut it out, you're driving me crazy!" I was so pent up and upset. Here was this little person coming at me and I couldn't strike out or hit; I just had to take it. So I would yell.

I was working ten or twelve hours a day before the divorce. Patti was home taking care of the house, packing us and moving us because we kept moving to bigger and better houses—we weren't taking time to love each other. I gave her no encouragement or appreciation. I had huge personal needs I wasn't sharing with her, and I felt she kept getting bossier and pushier. I only wanted to get away. And the crazy thing is, all Patti wanted was to make a wonderful home for us.

I knew I was a selfish person. Most of the things I did in my life I did because I was thinking only about me. If Patti didn't do what I wanted to do, I took it as an insult or as interference. I'd think, *What do I need this hassle for?*

And Patti always made me feel guilty for getting my own way. She'd pout and sulk or get sick, and I'd feel miserable.

I never perceived her as working hard for me or being the dutiful wife, like the childhood image I had of a wife. I just felt she was digging at me, nagging, trying to control me. I had been a married person since I was twenty-four years old. (Emotionally I was more like sixteen the first time I was married. I don't think I was ever ready for marriage at all.)

There came a day in July 1981 when I watched Patti come through the gate at the airport in Florida. I was doing a play there and she had been on tour with the musical *George M!* The heat was oppressive, heavy. Standing in the airport parking lot, I told her we were having dinner with friends, and her reaction didn't surprise me. She freaked out; she wanted us to spend time alone.

"After all, it's been a month since we've seen each other!" she argued.

I said to myself, *Why do I have to put up with this?*

In the car, the air conditioner was running, but no other sound could be heard. Then Patti asked me, accusingly, "What's the matter?"

"Nothing."

"Come on, Gavin, there's something the matter. Tell me what it is."

"*Nothing* is the matter. I'm just being quiet, that's all. Can't a person be quiet?"

"You're being quiet like a person who is *angry*. You're angry and upset! Tell me why you're angry and upset. *Answer* me."

I answered her! "Do you *really* want to know? I'll tell you what I'm upset about. I'll tell you what I'm angry about. These last few weeks I've been here in Florida alone without you have been the happiest weeks in my life."

"I don't believe it."

"You know something, Patti? We're so incompatible we can't even agree on what to argue about."

I had rented a little condo on the beach. I discovered I could walk on the sand as long as I wanted. I could be quiet and not talk if I chose. I could go to sleep when I wanted, eat when I wanted, wear what I wanted, buy what I wanted. Nobody asked who I was talking to on the telephone, or wanted a bite of my apple. Nobody queried me when I'd be home, where I was going, why I did what I did.

This was freedom. *Happiness,* I thought, *must be the freedom to do whatever you want without interference or questions or guilt.* For a man of fifty, I rationalized, who has worked hard his whole life, there ought to be some rewards. He should have something more to look forward to than a rocking chair on the porch and a nagging wife, shouldn't he? A man fifty years of age has a lot of life left in him, after all.

That's what I was thinking.

To me, women controlled things. When I was a kid my mother ran our house—even when my father was alive. My grandmothers, too, were the controllers, the ones who repaired the damage their husbands wrought. These men would tear up the world and the women came rushing and bustling in with brooms and dustpans to clean up the mess. I didn't want Patti cleaning up after me, ordering me to be a good boy. I didn't want my *mother* in my bed.

I didn't know that love is a skill and not just a feeling. I didn't know we could be *partners,* joint heirs, friends. I didn't know that by turning our lives over to God, we

Four generations. *Clockwise from front:* Me on my mother's knee, Great-Grandma Erickson, Grandma Shea.

Just after my first haircut.

A family portrait. *Clockwise from left:* Mom, Dad, me, Ronnie.

Patti's father, Lieutenant L.L. Kendig,
U.S. Navy, 1942.

Patti's mother, Margaret Kendig,
a beautiful woman whom she
adored.

Patricia Ann Kendig at
age twelve.

Theta Alpha Phi (photo from the 1951 *Cayugan*, Ithaca College Yearbook). That's me on the far right.

My Ithaca College graduation picture, 1952.

Cheerleading days (Patti on far right).

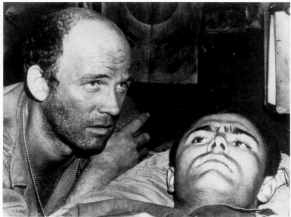

Early film roles. *Above left:* As a stuffy professor in *High Time* (1960).

Above right: A desperate soldier with John Saxon in *The War Hunt* (1961).

Right: A sadistic caliph in *Sword of Ali Baba* (1965).

Below: When I met Patti Steele, she was a single parent raising three children. *Left to right:* Drew, Patti, Stephanie, Tommy, Jr.

Patti and me with our children at our first wedding, George Washington's Birthday, 1974. *Front row, left to right:* Stephanie Steele, me, Patti, Meghan MacLeod, Keith MacLeod. *Top row, left to right:* Tommy Steele, David MacLeod, Julie MacLeod, Drew Steele.

Ed Asner as Lou Grant and the woebegone Murray on "The Mary Tyler Moore Show." (Notice the black sweater!)

Top left: A scene from my favorite episode of "The Love Boat." (ABC photograph.)

Top right: I was a samurai warrior in a dream sequence of "Love Boat" filmed in Japan. (ABC photograph.)

Above: Patti's fiftieth birthday party. Ethel Merman and Patti's daughter, Stephanie, help cut the cake. (New York *Daily News* photo.)

Right: Friend and co-star Marion Ross, me, and a bowl of sprouts for us dieters.

The L.A.D.I.E.S. group was good for Patti because the women were so supportive of one another.

Patti prayed for me and trusted God to answer.

June 30, 1985: A happy second wedding day.

Above left: The lady
who inspired my name:
Beatrice MacLeod, drama
teacher at Ithaca College.
Commencement, 1984.
(PHOTO BY Jon Crispin.)

Above right: Palm Springs,
1986. *Clockwise from front:*
My mother, my brother,
Ronnie, his wife, Anna ,
me, Patti.
(PHOTO BY Marie Chapian.)

Right: We're back on course
now — for good!

would be free of the bitterness and darkness that held us both in bondage and in a prison of self-seeking and pain.

So it was in Florida, with the July heat pressing down on us, that I told Patti, "I don't need you trying to control my life any longer." I didn't plan to say the things I said, I didn't want to say them, they just came out. We were taking a walk together and had sat down on a low wall that encircled the house. She said, "Well, I'll just go home then!"

I said, "Do whatever you want to do. I'm not telling you what to do."

So the next thing I knew, Patti was on her way to the airport to go back to Los Angeles, crying hysterically. All I knew was I liked the peace I was experiencing without her around. I *liked* being alone. It was new and fun to me. Without Patti there driving me crazy, maybe I could find peace.

Now that I was a free agent, navigating my own ship, sailing the high seas of life's beautiful adventures on my own, my children felt freer to move about in my life, to take part. But that meant they also saw me flopping about in stormy weather. I've always been a person who acts out his fantasies. I don't just dream and let it go at that. I go with it. I run with the dream. And at one time I thought those words were positive, "up" words: *Run with the dream, friend!* I had a storehouse of positive-thinking platitudes which I repeated constantly. I wanted everybody on the planet to be a winner. I wanted to strike out all the *un* words from the human vocabulary because they got in the way. I proclaimed that with up thoughts, nobody would ever steal your car and you'd always find a parking space. "Little hinges swing big doors," after all.

But life is deeper than that.

In September of 1981, "The Love Boat" finished filming a special musical segment with Ethel Merman, Ann Miller, and Carol Channing, and it was one of the highlights of the year. I especially loved that show, the music, the performances. After the last day of shooting, the producers threw a cast party at the Bistro Restaurant. It was the first major function I had to attend after the breakup, and I didn't have a date. At first I was tempted to call Patti and ask her to accompany me, but I thought, *I can't call her. We're getting a divorce.* I called my managers and we made up a list of available actresses to choose from. "That's how it's done in Hollywood. You can't be expected to attend these things without a date, after all," I was told. So I chose one of the actresses I had met briefly when she made an appearance on "The Love Boat." She agreed to the date, so I picked her up in my little white Volkswagen, and we pulled up at the restaurant in line with a string of limousines.

We sat chuckling as we watched actors and actresses, everybody on the show, climb out of their rented limos while we sat at the curb in the VW. There I was, the nearly single guy, expanding my world, realizing my full potential, experiencing new energies and vibrations—with an arranged date by my side, and not so much as the glitz of a limo to make an entrance in. Pretty funny!

I didn't worry about Patti reading the headlines and cover photos of the event in the *National Enquirer:* LOVE BUG BITES LOVE BOAT CAPTAIN. I was said to be madly in love and heading for the altar with my arranged date. That's show biz, right?

In 1982 "The Love Boat" went to Athens, the Greek Islands, Istanbul, Monte Carlo, Capri, Rome, and Venice. And I toured that summer in *High Button Shoes* on the strawhat circuit. In July "The Love Boat" sailed for the Orient—China, Hong Kong, Japan. The Japan sequence featured me as a shogun warrior. John Ritter, Linda Evans, John Forsythe, and my buddy Ted Knight were featured in the segments.

Our show now boasted over five hundred top star appearances since we went on the air. Most celebrity actors and actresses enjoyed working on "The Love Boat." The atmosphere and conditions were fabulous and we had fun. Ann Baxter said it was the best paid vacation she'd ever had.

Dennis Hammer, supervising casting director for the show, had a huge job on his hands. Every week he had to cast "six to eight recognizable faces" as well as big names. He had to be persistent when he went after certain people. One of my favorite stories is that in 1980, Dennis called the attorney of a famous forties movie star to do a guest appearance on "The Love Boat." The attorney said, "Are you aware that Governor Reagan is running for *president?*" Dennis Hammer replied, "Of course! Why do you think I'm calling?" The lawyer was not amused and told Dennis the governor was no longer interested in acting. Still hopeful, Hammer shot back, "How about Nancy?"

There was always joking among the cast members. We laughed a lot. I didn't know about Lauren Tewes' problem with cocaine until she came out with the story herself. I think she was really brave to admit her addiction and to go for help. Once she was free of the problem, she was back on the show. I gave her a big hug and congratulated her. I had overcome alcoholism, so I could appreciate her victory over drugs.

We did a segment about alcoholism on "The Love Boat" that was very close to my heart. Raymond Burr played an alcoholic on the show and as Captain Stubing I told him, "I licked booze and so can you." If you ever watch "The Love Boat," you'll see that the Captain *never* drinks. I was an alcoholic and so was the Captain. This segment was one of Aaron Spelling's favorites. He read me some of the letters from viewers: "Listen to this, Gavin: 'If the Captain can beat the battle with the bottle, I can, too.' "

So why wasn't I fulfilled? Why was I driven to work nearly every waking minute of my life? I put in ten or twelve hours a day on the set and then appeared in benefits, game shows, a Dean Martin roast, anything. I officiated at banquets, fund raisers for various good causes, and appeared in guest slots on television shows like "Hotel."

The best thing about those three years was the time I spent with my children. We became closer than we had ever been. I was all theirs, with nobody between us—except my work, and when the show went to Russia, Finland, Sweden, Paris, and London, I invited the kids along. It was one of the most adventurous experiences of our lives.

I didn't have a clue as to what was going on in Patti's life.
I didn't know and didn't bother to find out. The past was
past, to my way of thinking. Never look back, and all that.
Somebody once said, "Behind every famous man there's a
woman—telling him he's not so hot." I didn't want that in
my life.

Every year I was busier than the year before. My schedule was jammed. I was a recipient of the Man of the Year
Award, officiated in Omaha at the Annual Arthritis Benefit, was made an admiral in the Nebraska Navy, won the
Boys' Town Citizen of the Year Award.

In May 1984, "The Love Boat" presented its second gala
musical episode. In it I sang a ballad to my leading lady,
Alexis Smith. It wouldn't be until Marion Ross joined
the regular cast in the final year of taping that Captain
Stubing would have a real romance and not just passing
twangs of the series' cruise cupid. I made great friends
and worked with some of the most wonderful actors and
actresses in the world during the seven-year run of the
show.

But then something terrible happened. There I was, trying to find my younger self, when the bottom fell out. I got
news that my mother had a large tumor pressing on her

brain. If it stayed there it would kill her, but operating to remove it might kill her, too.

My brother and his wife, Anna, and their sons had moved to California from New York, and my mother lived with them. Anna was the one who broke the news about Mom to me. I was shattered. I didn't know how to pray, but I prayed anyhow—wildly, passionately. "Please, God, I'll do anything—I'll give up acting—please, just heal my mother. Don't let her die."

I pleaded with God, not knowing whether or not He was listening to me. What a devastating worry after all those years of thinking God and I were old pals.

Then one day while shooting "Love Boat" I received a note from Stephanie, Patti's daughter. It read, . . . *Gavin, you really ought to at least talk to my mother. She has totally changed. You wouldn't believe the difference. She's become a Born Again Christian.*

A what? I thought. *What does that mean?* I crumpled the letter. I'd *never* call Patti, not after all these years. No, I'd *never* call her!

I called her on the morning of September 27. I hadn't slept all night. My mother's surgery was that day and the prognosis was grim. I was frantic. It was a feeling of utter desolation and panic. In all the years I had lived away from home, I had known the security of her being there, her anchoring me to a time and a place. Mother, who was proud of her Allan but who never treated me like anything *but* Allan George See; never treated me like a Hollywood personality with a name like Gavin MacLeod, who cavorted around the world playing other people's lives.

I had sent Mom checks regularly through the years, bought her a condominium, telephoned, and brought her out to California for brief vacations before she moved there.

But all that seemed inadequate now. *She can't die, she can't die, she can't—*

"Hello Patti, it's Gavin. . . ."

She didn't seem shocked to hear from me. Her voice was happy, reassuring.

Yes, she'd pray. Yes, she'd like to see me. Sure, it would be great to get together this week. How about coming over for dinner in a couple of days? Nice to hear from you again, Gav. Take care. . . .

Patti and her Christian friends prayed nonstop for my mother. The surgery was a success! She recovered. It got me thinking about my life, about *God*.

Maybe seeing Patti again wasn't such a bad idea. . . .

PART TWO

PATTI

I'm just not the kind of person who gives up easily. The first time Gavin and I were married, in 1974, we decided on George Washington's birthday as an appropriate tribute to our hero. Besides, a numerologist told us it was a good day. We were into all sorts of sciences and beliefs at the time.

Ed and Nancy Asner gave a party at their home for the MTM cast to celebrate. Everyone on the show liked me, and I felt accepted and loved. Our friends realized that our relationship wasn't just a fling. They all wished us love and happiness.

Everybody in the wedding party wore red, white, and blue, and we asked our guests to wear the same. My bridal bouquet was of red, white, and blue flowers. Gavin wore a blue suit, a red-and-white-checked shirt, and navy blue knit tie.

The wedding was held at the Science of the Mind Church in Hollywood, and afterward the reception was held at the Cafe Alma, the MTM Friday night hangout.

I wore a Gunne Sax dress, the kind that was popular back in the seventies. It had leg-o'-mutton sleeves and an

ecru lace bodice with panels of pale blue lace all around.
My daughter, Stephanie, was my maid of honor. She wore
red, white, and blue, too, of course. My son Tommy drove
us to the church in his red Volkswagen. After the reception dinner, we fell apart, exhausted. The next day we
drove to Palm Springs for a honeymoon.

The important thing about the wedding was that we
were actually *doing it*. We were making the commitment.
That meant so much to me. We lived in a town where a
marriage was considered successful if the couple left the
church together. I felt sure that Gavin and I had a beautiful
future ahead of us.

We were both children of alcoholics; we lived and
worked in Hollywood; we were dreamers, deniers. It took
us so many years to find our way.

I was born Patricia Ann Kendig on March 8, 1931, the only child of Margaret Elizabeth and Lester Lee Kendig. After nine years of waiting, I was the baby my parents had dreamed of having. My father was in the Naval Reserve and worked for the Treasury Department. My mother, petite and sensitive, was a navy stenographer and a yeomanette. We lived on Buchanan Street in Washington, D.C., in a tidily kept row house with a fully equipped and spotlessly clean nursery I still remember.

My father was a handsome navy man from a Protestant background, and my mother was a nice Catholic girl who graduated from Immaculate Conception, an all-girl high school. Both were born and raised in Washington, D.C. What my mother wanted most in life was a husband and child of her own, a family that was all hers, and a place where she belonged. Daddy came from a large family and didn't realize the deep need Mother had. Her mother had died when she was twelve, after which her father took off, never to be heard from again. Aunt Gertie, her mother's sister, took charge. To my thirty-two-year-old mother, I was an answer to prayer.

I became my father's little "cream puff." I was pampered and fussed over like a delicate work of art. And delicate I was. I was never a really robust child. I seemed to catch every ailment that came along and always had the worst case the doctor had seen. But I had a natural joy and enthusiasm for life. I suppose you could say I was spoiled and pampered, but I got along well with my friends and grown-ups alike.

Our house on Buchanan Street always smelled of lemon oil, Ivory Flakes, and Clorox. Mother liked things clean and taught me the same virtues. I was so clean all the time, I could be dressed up in all my pretty little ruffles, go outside and play in a mudhole, and not get a spot on myself. My father was the original Mr. Fixit, and nothing was broken around our house for more than five minutes.

Mother sang and played the piano beautifully and when friends dropped by, they gathered around and sang the latest hits. I would sit on the piano bench beside her, swinging my legs and clapping my hands in delight to songs like "The Music Goes Round and Round" and "Red Sails in the Sunset."

Friends always dropped by at night for tea and dessert; people made their own fun then. We were a happy family and friends liked coming to our house. I spent my days under the loving eye of Mother, braiding clover chains while sitting cross-legged in the soft, cool grass with my playmates, and having tea parties for my dolls. But the big event of the day was Daddy's coming home from work. Mother and I got all prettied up for that moment. Evenings were spent sitting on Daddy's lap being read to or listening to our favorite programs on the radio.

Aunt Gertie, who raised my mother and lived with us, sewed like a professional seamstress and produced, almost magically, little beaver muffs with matching beaver hats, dress-and-cape sets, ruffled dresses with miles of skirt and petticoat, and embroidered blouses and dresses for me. A friend of Mother worked at a department store and bought me six dresses every Christmas. I was the Shirley Temple of Buchanan Street.

Every week Mother prayed before the statue of the Blessed Mother to be a good wife to her husband and a good mother to her child. She had made it her life's work to please my daddy and give us a beautiful home. Aunt Gertie did all the cooking and Mother did all the cleaning. She *loved* to clean.

Aunt Gertie died in 1935, and later that year we moved to a new home at 5224 First Street. To Mother it was a dream come true. She loved fireplaces, and this house had two of them. Her beautiful walnut living-room furniture stood slipcovered for the summer so the dust and humidity wouldn't harm it. Everything was so clean and neat and happy.

I attended St. Gabriel's Catholic School, and on Sundays Mother and I attended mass at St. Gabriels' Church. Daddy didn't go to church, even though he had converted to Catholicism when he married Mother.

I was loved by Mommy and Daddy. I had the sense of belonging and being a person who was very, very special.

I hated most foods and I spent hours too numerous to count sitting at the dining-room table long after dinner was over, staring at a full plate of food. "I hate beans. I hate lettuce. I hate gravy. I hate yukky ishy peas and carrots." (I didn't eat vegetables until I moved to Delaware with my first husband, when we ate farm-fresh produce. I'm certainly making up today for my early lack of appetite.)

To Mother, *good* was a word of immense value and power. She had to be a *good* wife, a *good* mother, a *good* singer, a *good* housekeeper, a *good* cook, and she taught me the power of *good*, too.

I was Daddy's *good* little girl. I was admonished to clean my room *good*, in order to be a *good* girl. I was a *good* girl for going to piano and dancing lessons. I learned that *good* meant getting and keeping the approval of the people around me.

My father made holidays something magical. He never let an occasion for a celebration pass unnoticed. On Easter he took me to the White House lawn for the Easter Egg Hunt; on the Fourth of July we went to the Lincoln Memorial to watch the fireworks; on birthdays we had picnics and parties. And Christmas was the most wonderful event of the year. Both Mommy and Daddy worked hard at making it special. My dolls would disappear one by one until on Christmas morning they all reappeared dressed in new dresses. There were presents and decorations and music. The house would be filled with friends. We sang and sang and the enormous Christmas tree scraping the ceiling would be ablaze with colored balls and lights.

So what could have been wrong with this happy childhood picture? My father was an alcoholic. No matter how happy and cozy your world is, if there's an alcoholic in the picture, there's a crack in it somewhere. He was never violent, but I could sense something wrong by the way he slurred his words or made amorous remarks to my mother. I often felt a panic that I couldn't understand or explain— that something terrible was happening.

A Washington row house is attached to another house on either side. Ours had a beautiful back garden Mother planted and tended to. I loved the lilacs and hydrangeas, and every summer when the roses and pansies blossomed, Mother filled vases of them throughout the house. Our

garden had snapdragons, crocuses, tulips, bachelor buttons, and Washington's famous azaleas. It seemed the entire universe was ablaze in color and life when the garden
came alive. Summers were uniquely special, and when
Daddy was away with the Reserve, mother and I made the
best of it until he was home again. I felt safe and happy
when Daddy was home.

When summer came, it seemed as if it would never end.
Time stopped and the days were long and wonderful. I
rode my bike, played jacks, kick-the-can, and hide-and-
go-seek with the neighborhood gang. We waited for the
Good Humor truck, and when we ate our ice-cream pops,
it was as if we'd never finish them. The neighbors sat on
their porches visiting back and forth. We drank lemonade,
watching the sun set over the rooftops. Sometimes Mother
ordered ice cream from the drugstore and the delivery boy
would bring it in the hand-packed box just as the edges
were beginning to melt. There would always be this time;
these roses in the vase would always be here; we'd always
have ice cream and lemonade—and be loved.

I never missed a Shirley Temple movie, and Mother
sang and played all the new songs. She loved books and
gave me a love for reading. She loved clothes, too, and
taught me how to dress and appreciate beautiful clothes.
(There was a Franciscan monastery near us, and I was
crushed when I found out I couldn't be a monk because I
loved their wonderful flowing robes and big wooden crosses
and sandals.)

My life was happy and innocent then.

That's why, on December 7, 1941, it came as such a
shock when the Japanese bombed Pearl Harbor. The news
devastated our home because my father was in the Naval

Reserve and was called back into active duty as a lieutenant commander.

Suddenly Mother and I were alone. She didn't want me to see her fear, so she tried to keep a cheerful face when I was around. She told me wonderful stories of how Daddy was a hero and he would be sending for us soon. We sang "Over There" at the piano.

"My daddy's an officer fighting for our country!" I boasted to the neighborhood children. "He's sending for us soon."

He was my handsome, strong daddy, who held me on his lap, took me to the movies and to the drugstore for ice cream. I missed his charm, his strength, his sounds, and his smells. With him gone things didn't seem safe.

But weeks turned into months and Mother's countenance became more and more drawn. Her eyes were red and swollen most of the time, and she lost interest in music and playing the piano. She complained about lack of money. I heard her fretting over not being able to pay the orthodontist for the braces on my teeth. I didn't want Mother to worry or be upset, and I tried to comfort her.

"Daddy will send for us soon, Mama, won't he? Please don't cry."

But he didn't send for us. There were no more vacations in Atlantic City with Daddy, no more trips like the one to the World's Fair, when we stayed at the Taft Hotel. It was so quiet now. Mother had sheltered me from knowing the truth until she could hide it no longer. Her best friend, whom I call Aunt Elsie, convinced her to stop lying to me; I had a right to know. My father was stationed in Miami, Florida. He had met another woman, twenty years his junior. One month after he left home he had written to Mother asking for a divorce.

"I'm sorry, honey, but your daddy's not ever going to send for us—and he's never coming back."

Mother never recovered from the shock of what he had done. One minute he was standing at the front door with tears in his eyes, telling her he loved her and hugging his little girl, assuring us we'd be together soon, and one month later he was in love with another woman. Gone forever.

The light in Mother's eyes went out and never returned. She had to leave the home she loved so much and go back to work after ten years. She began drinking, and my happy little world was no more. Daddy married the twenty-one-year-old woman.

I lay thinking in my bed at night, staring at the wallpaper with little pink and blue angels and moons: *What happened to my daddy? Doesn't he love me anymore? It's because I wasn't good. Now I must be very, very good because then Mommy won't miss Daddy so much. If she doesn't miss him so much, she won't drink. Then my daddy will come back.*

It was nearly a year later when Mother told me I had to go to Miami to visit Daddy.

"Are you coming, too, Mommy?"

"No, honey. It's in the divorce agreement that you go to visit him two weeks every summer."

"But I don't want to go alone. I want you to come."

"I can't."

"Then I won't go either!"

"You must. He's your father."

The hurt I felt as an eleven-year-old was almost unbearable. I had to hang onto Mother to keep her from drinking. I wanted to be able to make her happy so she wouldn't hurt herself. "No!" I sobbed. "I won't leave you!"

I believed I had to convince her that I didn't miss Daddy

at all—that I loved only her. I thought if Mommy knew that, maybe she would be happy. Maybe she would stop drinking. "The pain of a broken heart is far greater than the pain of a broken bone," I had heard Ma Perkins say on the radio. My loyalty to Mother was so fierce, I couldn't dare allow myself to love my father.

But I was sent to Florida to visit him. He met me at the Miami airport and took me to the beach with his wife, a flawless beauty whom he romped with like a love-struck teenager. He was happier than I had ever seen him, and more handsome, if that was possible. I had been proud of him, but not now. He tried to make my visit a fun one, but I remained sullen and distant. I realized the nightmare was real. He wasn't coming home. Ever.

I had taken dancing lessons from age five. Now I began to think all those years studying dance with Miss Madelaine and Miss Lila were a waste. "Mama, I don't want to be in the May Ball anymore and I don't care how many solos I get."

"But you're so good at toe and tap now, and your acrobatics—"

"I want to be a *real* dancer."

"There's some other kind?"

"I don't think Miss Madelaine is a real dancer. She's *fat*, Mama. And she doesn't wear the right things."

Mother looked puzzled.

"I know what the real thing is now. I was over at Carol's house, and her older sister Marjorie is a ballet dancer at the Washington School of Ballet. There she was, Mama, standing and eating an apple and reading a book with her leg up on top of the refrigerator."

I was fourteen when I started classes at the Washington School of Ballet across town. It was a dream come true! It was my first *real* dance training. I took ballet classes, attended Calvin Coolidge High School, never missed a cheerleading practice, always finished my homework, got straight *A*s (except a *D* in Geometry once), and started dating boys.

Mother was drinking more and I never knew what condition she'd be in when I came home. I tried to make sure friends didn't come over until I was certain Mother was sober enough not to embarrass herself . . . or me.

I had a weak constitution and was perpetually nervous. I couldn't handle pressure well. The trials of adolescence, high school life, dating for the first time, *and* an alcoholic mother almost did me in, but I stuck my chin out at the world and refused to give up.

We had moved out of the house in our old neighborhood to 113 Hawaii Avenue because we couldn't afford the payments. I had felt security and love in the house on First Street in a neighborhood with people who had known me since I was four. Now I began experiencing some of the empty, panicked feelings similar to those when my father walked out. But I was determined, for Mother's sake, to make the best of it.

I shared a bedroom with Mother and I didn't mind the arrangement because then I could watch her more carefully. I began to worry about every minute I spent away from her. I worried that something terrible would happen if I wasn't there. When I went out in the evenings I called at least two or three times to make sure she wasn't drinking. I could tell from the sound of her voice if she had drunk even one sip.

Mother could tell I was overworking and overdoing, so she arranged a vacation to Chicago for the two of us. We took the train and visited Aunt Anne and Uncle Pete and their family—Uncle Pete was my father's brother. I was thrilled at the idea and began planning what to pack, what to wear, and what kinds of things would be fun to do in

Chicago. On the day we were to leave, Mother was too drunk to get on the train. She practically had to be carried on board, and after that the vacation was ruined for me. The worst thing about living with an alcoholic, I learned, was that you never knew when to expect the bomb to drop. Mother would go weeks, sometimes months, without a drink, and everything would be fine. No incidents. Then without warning, I would come home from school or dance class to find her passed out or drunk. When she drank, her appearance changed. An attractive, mild-mannered woman turned careless, inarticulate, belligerent.

I became obsessed with trying to keep her from drinking. Often on Saturdays, instead of going out with my friends, I spent all day and all night with her. I'd plan a downtown shopping trip or a movie and dinner, keeping my eye on Mother every second so she wouldn't drink. I even followed her into the ladies' room. But it didn't make any difference. If I spent twenty-three hours and fifty-nine minutes a day with her, there would be that one minute she could sneak a drink. It drove me crazy.

I took various jobs for short periods of time, as a salesgirl at Garfinkle's in the jewelry department, as a receptionist at Commerce Clearing House, as a clerical worker in a real estate office. I baby-sat and held various temporary office jobs.

I was happy at school or at work, and most of all, at ballet class. My teachers, Lisa Gardner and Mary Day, were the epitome of grace and glamour. Miss Gardner wore her gray curls piled high on her head and carried a long cigarette holder; her two Bedlington terriers trotted alongside her. And Miss Day was a striking woman of intense drama and beauty, beguiling her young students into total dedication to the rigorous life of the ballerina.

At Calvin Coolidge I was popular and everyone liked me. I went to all the dances, and as a cheerleader, never missed a sports event. I faithfully attended mass every Sunday with my Mother and looked forward to it. I don't remember a time in my life when I didn't hunger for God. I dreamed of going to New York to be a dancer, but how could I leave my mother?

I met Tom Steele, a good-looking University of Maryland student, at the beach one summer day. He began showing up at our house with friends, and soon we were dating. On our dates, I dutifully called home to check on Mother. "Have you been drinking?" I'd ask, and Mother couldn't figure out how I could tell. She was such a loving mother, so much fun. Except for her drinking, she was the perfect mother. She made a beautiful home for us. That's why it was so hard for me to see her hurt herself by drinking.

It undercut my own feelings of self-worth. I never felt really pretty in my whole life, but in high school I felt special because I had my dancing, something of my *own*; it was mine, and nobody else in my crowd did what I did. But I was eager to leave home.

I married the handsome Tom Steele on April 28, 1951, when I was twenty. We moved to Rehoboth Beach, Delaware, into a tiny apartment which my mother hated. It was so difficult being away from her, but I was starry-eyed and in love and I had my very own home. Tom and I had three incredibly beautiful children before we moved from Delaware to California in 1958.

Tommy, Jr., was born September 12, 1953; Stephanie Anne was born December 12, 1954; and Andrew Kenton was born August 6, 1957. I was a married lady and a mother, but what should have been another perfect life, wasn't. My dream of being a dancer ended, and the love of tradition my mother had given me was ended, too. No more happy excursions to the countryside and eating fresh, hot biscuits with melted butter in country inns; no more Sunday dinners with a houseful of friends singing around the piano, and sitting up late together reading Daphne du Maurier . . . and I found myself in an unhappy marriage.

In December 1960, we were living in Santa Monica, a western suburb of Los Angeles. I missed my mother and wanted her to come out and live with us, but she insisted on staying in Washington, D.C.: it was her home, after all. She had her job with the Department of the Interior, her friends, Aunt Elsie, her apartment; she didn't want to be dependent. Besides, I was busy with three children of my own. But I wanted her right under my nose where I could watch her and make sure she was okay. I knew she was still drinking heavily. Once she had admitted, reluctantly, that she could *possibly* have some alcoholic tendencies.

Mother was healthy and feeling good and that was a relief. But on a Thursday night in December 1960, she went Christmas shopping with Aunt Elsie; they took the bus downtown, had dinner in a restaurant, and then did a little shopping because the stores were open late on Thursday night. They took the bus back home.

Mother said good-night to Aunt Elsie, walked into her apartment building, took the elevator to her floor, and collapsed. A neighbor found her lying at the doorway of her apartment with her rosary in her hand. The contents of her purse were spread out on the floor, where she had frantically groped for her rosary.

I received a call with the message that Mother had suffered a severe stroke and was in the hospital in a coma. It was snowing on the eastern seaboard, and Christmas travelers had booked every flight to Washington, D.C. The only available flight was on Saturday morning. I called the hospital, and Mother's doctor said if she lived, she would be brain dead. I couldn't repeat his words.

Frantic, I boarded the plane at the Los Angeles airport in the press of holiday travelers, leaving Tom to take care of the children. I could hardly think or see straight. Tears flowed, and I made no attempt to hold them back. I believed if I could get there, everything would be okay. Doctors often make mistakes. Mother could rally. I could see her face with that look of private suffering.

Due to the storm conditions, the plane was forced to land in Detroit. We could be delayed from twelve to twenty-four hours, they said. I was nearly hysterical when a kindly man who had sat next to me on the flight from Los Angeles offered to help me get a train out of Detroit that would take me to Silver Spring, Maryland. The airport was a cacophony of stranded, exhausted, and frustrated people. Babies were crying; whole families were crouched on top of luggage on the floor; crowds too dense to penetrate had descended on every ticket counter. Crying and numb with fear, I followed the man outside to the taxi stand.

It looked as if the entire city of Detroit was waiting for a taxi, bus, or anything that moved. Snow had delayed and stopped traffic, and it seemed there would be no way to get across town to the railroad station. But somehow we did it. I tried to be gracious to the man who was being so helpful and understanding.

The train we boarded smelled musty with age, and the

aisle creaked as we moved to our seats. It looked like vintage Jessie James. The snowstorm didn't let up, and the train seemed to barely inch along the tracks. I was wearing only a light dress with a spring coat over it, and high heels.

My father's brother, Uncle Norman, met me at Silver Spring. How did he know I was on that train? I didn't want to look at him in the eye, didn't want to see his face. His expression would tell me Mother's condition. It would be right there in his face. And I was right. His eyes darted back and forth nervously. His mouth was drawn, uncomfortable. *Don't say it*, I thought. *I want to see my mother right away. Just take me to my mother.*

". . . I'm sorry, Patricia. Your mother passed away this morning."

There were people to talk to, the funeral home arrangements, flowers. It was Sunday, and there was a strong, cold wind blowing across the empty streets, the statues in the parks, the circles. Monday I sat next to the casket as people came to pay their respects. I was like a child lost in a department store. Everything was gigantic, confusing. There was only one face I looked for, one familiar voice, one pair of arms I longed to be held out to me.

A letter arrived at the funeral home addressed to me. I sat in the stillness, wondering why it was so quiet, like being stuffed in a box of cotton. People came to pay their respects. It seemed everyone I had ever known in my whole life was there. People who were old when I was young were there. And my mother was only sixty-one years old—gone. I opened the letter, recognizing the name with a gasp: L.L. Kendig.

I read it and then crumpled it in my fist. My father wrote, . . . *your mother was the only woman I ever loved.*

Later, sorting through Mother's belongings with Aunt Elsie, I thought, *He ruined my mother's life, ruined mine—I heard he's had four wives. And when mother is lying there dead in the casket, he sends a bolt out of the past . . . but doesn't even show up.* I suddenly felt tired, very tired.

I didn't have the feeling of being special or important anymore. When I married Tom I wanted to bring a smile to his beautiful face. I never did. My children gave me the warmth and love I craved, and I lavished affection on them, but I felt a sense of emptiness now. Life to me was nerve-racking, enervating, and demanding. I never knew when the bottom might fall out. I hungered for something more.

Once I had been a dancer and had big dreams for a sparkling tomorrow. Now where was my dream? Where was my happily-ever-after family? My anxiety and distress put me in a state of collapse, and I was hospitalized. I was told this was a nervous breakdown. Several more years of unhappiness followed before my marriage to Tom ended in 1967.

I was active in the Catholic church until my divorce. I created musical evenings that became quite popular with the parishioners. When I filed for divorce, however, I was no longer allowed to be active in any outreach or group in the church. Feeling utterly abandoned by the faith of my childhood, I threw my energies into the occult, where I was accepted without question.

There was no lack of occult groups in the Los Angeles area. I was angry at the Catholic church, so I went to hear the maharishis and the gurus. I delved for the past lives everyone was talking about. I went to Unity to find out how I fit into some sort of universal pattern of existence. I tried communicating with positive energies. I experimented with discovering the universal extension of self and tried to see myself in the absence of adversity. It was a vain effort. Adversity was my middle name.

Christian Science promised health and perfection, whereas spiritualism offered proof of survival after death through seances and the secret keys to contacting dead loved ones. I tried to find the "ever-present 'I Am,' filling all space, including in itself all Mind, the one Father-Mother God," that Mary Baker Eddy taught. I studied Divine Science, which was supposed to be the same as the Spirit of God; then the impersonal God of Theosophy and its seven plains leading to a Theosophist's heaven.

I tried numerology, the scientific study of numbers, in order to try to direct my life and predict the future. I tried Science of the Mind because it taught that God and self were one and the same, and if I visualized what I wanted, I could have it because God already had it all. I thought all I had to do was plug into my "God self."

Hindu beliefs had me looking for deity in all existence. I read my horoscope and had my charts done. I tried to get rid of tensions and inhibitions with rebirthing. I went to psychics for advice and gave up eating meat. I got in touch by Rolfing, strange elixirs and herbs from the Orient, and meditation. But I was still out of touch.

Finally, I was taken to a doctor in San Juan Capistrano, who put me on a diet of natural foods and changed my life.

After the divorce, the three children—Tommy, Jr., Stephanie, and Andrew—and I lived in a little home in Santa Monica next to Elizabeth Taylor and her husband, Dr. Wendell Taylor. Not *the* Elizabeth Taylor but our own Elizabeth Taylor. She and her husband became our new "family."

I was unsure of the future. I lived in a town that extolled

fame and success, no matter how fleeting or meaningless. Hollywood, Neil Simon once said, is Paradise with a lobotomy. In Hollywood there are those people addicted to fame and illusion. Many of these Hollywood residents are not stars, but they have the pursuit of the illusion ingrained in their thinking and could not, would not, dare to change lest the loss of illusion take away their very self.

It was difficult to survive such an environment. I wasn't a star, and in my opinion, I wasn't a success at anything. So what was I? I had failed with my mother; I had failed with my husband. I had not failed with my children, thank God. I was thirty-five years old. What could I do well? Would anyone ever love me again?

Like my mother, I had to leave my home and children and go to work. My first jobs were clerical. Someone suggested my children ought to be in commercials because they were so all-American looking. My friend Suzanne had all my children signed to Bill Cunningham, a new commercial agent in town, and they started working like crazy. They loved it, and it kept us close together.

I didn't meet Gavin MacLeod until five years later. Next to him every man I had ever known was boring. I made lots of friends whom I loved, but I seemed to attract the kind of guy who lights up a room when he *leaves*. Gavin was fireworks! He was technicolor in a black-and-white world.

When I first met Gavin I was surprised at how big he is. He didn't look that big on TV. He was *fat*—close to 270 pounds. Gavin is one of the few people who look thinner on television. Being a dancer, I was always attracted to athletic types, but I was attracted to Gavin, the most unathletic person I'd ever known.

I started teaching tap dancing at the Words and Music

workshop on Saturday mornings. Gavin came, trying to learn shuffle-hop-step and disrupting the class. But I thought he was funny. After the class we'd all go out together for something to eat. We were rehearsing *A Funny Thing Happened on the Way to the Forum*, and our spirits were always high. Gavin would drink, and he'd be funny and we'd all laugh at him. I never saw him become mean or nasty in those days, so his drinking seemed under control. But then one Saturday Valerie Harper had a party, and we were both invited. We had a rehearsal earlier at the workshop, and Gavin asked me if I'd like to ride with him in his car. At the party I watched him get drunker and drunker. I could see real problems.

Gavin invited my children and me to "The Mary Tyler Moore Show" taping on Friday nights. They did the show before a live audience, and it was like going to the theatre. Pretty soon people could tell we were serious about each other. Valerie Harper was so sweet to me. She thought Gavin and I were meant for each other right from the beginning.

In 1973 Gavin played in the musical *Gypsy* with Kaye Ballard in San Diego. It was the beginning of a long and warm friendship among the three of us. Kaye told me I was like a tonic to Gavin. But he had some bad drinking scenes and I thought, *Sure I'm a tonic—like the kind that comes in a beer can.*

I figured I could fix things up, though. I thought I could just love him so much he'd change. It was the same way it had been with my mother. I just *had* to help make everything okay. Well, Gavin was wonderful in *Gypsy* and so was Kaye. She's a great talent. After *Gypsy* closed, Kaye opened in Reno with her nightclub act. She invited us up to see the show and then stay over for a little vacation.

Gavin had a week off from "The Mary Tyler Moore Show," so we drove up. Kaye was staying in a gorgeous suite on the eighteenth floor of her hotel. Some of her other friends were there, and she had rented rooms for everybody. It was wonderful until the last night. Gavin hadn't had a drink for three months. Kaye doesn't drink at all, I don't drink, and Kaye's friends didn't drink much.

On the last night Gavin had "one little drink" which turned into "many little drinks." Kaye had never seen him this way. Driving to our hotel later he was like a wild man. I said, "Stop the car, Gavin. I'm getting out." He refused. So I told him, "If you don't stop the car I'm going to jump out." When we got to the hotel, we were screaming at each other, not caring who heard us.

Poor Kaye was in shock. I said I was flying back to Los Angeles in the morning. I loved him but couldn't put myself or my children in a position to be hurt again. He said in his drunken slur, "I don't care what you do. I'm Indian and I drink. If you don't like it, there are lots of women just waiting to take your place." That hurt.

"Gavin, you have to stop saying that. It's cruel and unkind!" Finally I said that I was leaving him. I would not be married to an alcoholic!

I didn't sleep much that night, and when I woke up in the morning Gavin was sitting on the edge of my bed. He was crying. He said to me, "Patti, I've never said this to another person in my entire life. . . ." It was awkward to see him crying, and I wondered what was going on. Then he said, "I'm so ashamed about last night.

"Patti, I mean this—I will never take another drink as long as I live."

Now he had my full attention. I sat straight up.

"Last night you said you would leave me, and I don't want to lose you," he said. "You're the best thing that's ever happened to me."

I didn't know how to react. I knew something had happened inside his heart. I thanked God for this miracle. I told him I didn't want to leave him either, and that I would do anything in the world to help him. But I had lived with alcoholism so many years of my life, I couldn't take another minute of watching another loved one go down the tubes.

Incredibly, Gavin kept his promise. He has not had a drink from that day to this.

But, here's the catch. He never went to Alcoholics Anonymous, which I thought was important. He stopped drinking but he still had an alcoholic personality. He continued to call me names, insult me, and he was *full* of anger. I would tell myself, *Oh, he doesn't really mean that. He* couldn't *mean that*, but he did mean it. If he got angry at anything out of the house or with some person or situation, he'd take it out on me. I accepted that kind of behavior, thinking that one day the anger would go away. Being the child of an alcoholic, I still wanted to believe I could help change him. He stopped drinking but he wasn't truly healed until Christ touched and healed him years later. We both had a long way to go until then. We had to get married, get divorced, and get married again.

Most Hollywood wives receive cars, pearls, jewels as wedding gifts from their grooms. Gavin gave me a puppy.

So on our wedding night we had our puppy in the hotel room at the Riviera Hotel in Palm Springs. Gavin fell asleep right away, and there I was, cleaning up after my present all night. We named him "Elton," after Elton John. He was adorable, like the RCA dog, all white with one eye ringed in black. He was the cutest thing as a puppy, but Elton grew up to look just like a little pig.

On our honeymoon in Palm Springs we went for long walks, rode bicycles, ate health foods. I hoped to goodness I had done the right thing. Our friend Kaye Ballard had a place in town, so the three of us palled around with little ring-eyed Elton in tow. Kaye gave a party in our honor. "I love Palm Springs so much, I hope we can live here someday," I told her.

"Good," Kaye answered. "I'll start looking immediately."

I sold my little house in Santa Monica and Gavin and I bought a house in the seaside community of Pacific Palisades on Las Casas. I thought it was the worst house in the world. I hated that house. It was right on the street.

There was the tiniest sidewalk and then the house, right there on the street. So I'd be at the kitchen sink and I could practically read the speedometers of the cars as they went by.

Downstairs were two bedrooms and another huge room. We never went down there. Then there was another level with a large living room with a fireplace and a photographer's darkroom. There was a garden outside. We never went out there. We had absolutely crazy next-door neighbors.

Then, to top it all off, Gavin's old buddy from New York, Jimmy Downey, moved in with us. He moved in with his cigar hanging from his teeth, drinking his beer, and it was not the most romantic time. Jimmy was like the man who came to dinner.

Moving got to be a thing with us. We have looked for the perfect house, the "dream house," all our lives. Gavin loved houses, *loved* them. I went along with him. The next house we bought in Palisades was beautiful except again we had weird neighbors. We called them Mr. and Mrs. Hitler. Gavin and I would come home from a Friday night shoot of "The Mary Tyler Moore Show," and it would be very late because sometimes they didn't finish until eleven or twelve o'clock at night. The whole group of us—Valerie, Ed and Nancy, Ted and Dottie, Georgia—would go out to dinner, a very quiet dinner because everyone was exhausted. Then Gavin and I would drive home, so it might be one-thirty or two o'clock in the morning. We'd pull in the driveway and Mr. Hitler would jump out of the bushes and announce, "Your dog is barking."

Scary. So we'd go inside and Elton would be sound asleep under the bed. The children and I had two other dogs named Bow and Arrow, who were also asleep. We put the house up for sale. It sold the first day it was on the market.

Our next house was in Sherman Oaks, a community north of Beverly Hills and the Stone Canyon Reservoir. Jimmy Downey was no longer with us. He had left in a strange way. We found a note on the hall table. It said, *When you read this, I'll be dead.* Gavin panicked. Jimmy was one of his oldest friends. We tried to find him, called all his favorite haunts and everyone who knew him, but there were no clues. Gavin was devastated. "It's just not like Jimmy," he said. "He's not the suicide type." He called the Los Angeles police, the hospitals, the sheriff, but there was no sign of Jimmy.

Gavin worried himself sick. He's not good in crisis situations. He couldn't believe a tough little Irishman like Jimmy Downey could commit suicide.

We didn't hear one word from Jimmy for several years. Then one day Gavin was walking down Third Avenue in New York, looked in the window of a restaurant, and there was Jimmy at the cash register. He was managing the place and just never thought to let us know he was okay.

I have always said Gavin isn't one to sit around idly wasting time. His mother tells how, if her Allan wasn't busy with something when he was a boy, she figured he had a fever or was deathly sick. He still isn't good at relaxing. He deals with his worries by getting busier. He never likes to sit down and think about things that are painful.

When the cast had time off from their heavy schedule rehearsing and shooting "The Mary Tyler Moore Show," Gavin worked on other shows. In 1976 he appeared on "The Donny and Marie Show" and was impressed with the talent and genuine hometown sweetness of the eighteen-year-old Donny and sixteen-year-old Marie.

That same year Gavin and I formed a nightclub act together. Gavin wanted to do musicals, and I was thrilled to perform with him. Gavin's career had skyrocketed while mine hadn't really begun. After eight months of writing and developing the act and four weeks of rehearsals, we opened on March 19, 1976, in Houston at the Million Dollar City Dump, with a song by Johnny Bradford:

GAVIN (*singing*) Mind if I say you're cute?
PATTI I am so sick of being cute—I've been cute all my life.
GAVIN (*singing*) I really mean you're cute . . .
PATTI Well, I was the Doris Day of my neighborhood, little Peter Pan all through college—
GAVIN (*singing*) I mean, I like your style . . . your sly, intriguing smile . . .
PATTI Oh, I was a cheerleader, too.
GAVIN (*singing*) Your every mood, your attitude, just add up to— you're cute!

Gavin told friends it was a nightclub act you could bring the children to. The costumes were by Pete Menefee (assistant to the famous Bob Mackie); Roland Dupree choreographed; the conductor traveling with us was Bob Bailey; and to round out the act, three dancer-singers, Nikki D'Amico, Joey Sheck, and Tom Callas, provided backup and joined in the production numbers. Like the opening number, "Gavin Mac Who?"

SINGERS Autograph! Autograph! Say, isn't that Mr. MacGavin?
GAVIN (*entering stage left*) Wait a minute. Let's get this straight. Say it out loud. The name's *MacLeod*. (*singing*) That's Gavin MacLeod not Darren McGavin; not Mr. McQueen or Mr. Clean or Marshall McLuhan or Mr. McGovern or Mac MacMillan, or Ed McMahon—it's *Gavin MacLeod!* Say it out loud.

Vintage nostalgia, pizzazz, and show tunes—the act opened with an audio tape of Ted Knight introducing his old friend "Gavin McDarrin—or is it—?" The *Houston Chronicle* critic loved the show and said:

> One of the funniest sketches I've seen in ages is a bicen-
> tennial number with Gavin and wife, Patti, in which they
> portray Betsy Ross and her mythical hubby, Bruce. Gavin
> had the audience in the palm of his hand. . . . The loveliest
> thing about the show is Gavin's warmth and rapport with
> his audience. Whether he's singing, dancing, or just talk-
> ing. . . . Patti is a talented warbler-dancer, a knockout on
> the tune "Nothing" from *A Chorus Line.*

Variety called the act "a nice example of the 'personality' act, a smooth-running, undemanding vehicle for an instantly recognizable, likable performer . . ." and oh, yes, "MacLeod's wife, Patti, did a nice job with a number from *A Chorus Line.*"

We were on the road—first Houston, then Minneapolis, Denver, New York. It was a charming show. But when the producers tried to make us Las Vegas, it just didn't work. We developed another act when Gavin was in "The Love Boat" because Gavin loves to work, and we opened that one in Dallas. Then we played San Francisco. Our managers, the audiences, everybody told us we were great together—"You just spark each other"—but when we played San Francisco, something starting falling apart.

Little by little, I knew people were telling Gavin to dump me. To my face it was, "Hello, sweetie, *love* your show," but behind my back it was, "Gavin, get rid of Patti and we can put you in Vegas with female dancers behind you, like John Davidson."

I started doubting my own talent. I knew I wouldn't be on that stage if it weren't for Gavin. I knew people paid to see Gavin, not me. But I wanted to believe I was good, so I waited for Gavin to defend me. But he never did. We were sitting at a table in the Fairmont, and two very catty young men were telling Gavin how wonderful he was and how much the audiences loved him, and I felt myself shrinking. When we got to our room I went to pieces. "You don't say a single word to defend me, not a word!" And Gavin thought I was persecuting him, railing at him.

We closed in San Francisco and it was downhill after that. Our material didn't work. It was good material, it just wasn't for us. Some people were supportive, and I appreciated that. Gavin's manager told me, "Something happens to Gavin when you come on that stage, Patti. It's like magic. You really have electricity between you." But others were cruel.

When you have ungodly people in an ungodly situation, ungodly things are going to happen. You're going to have ungodly feelings and relationships. And we were smack in the middle of an ungodly world, where marriage was looked upon as something tacky. It seemed I didn't know one person who saw the value in a family on stage together.

One of Gavin's numbers from our act, "That Old Straw Hat My Father Wore," particularly touched audiences. It was a song which spoke of his father being in vaudeville and now he, the son, was wearing his straw hat. One night Joey Bishop was in the audience and he told Gavin, "I didn't know your father was in vaudeville. I saw that number and cried like a baby."

Gavin did the number on "The Mike Douglas Show" and then he appeared in a summer replacement for "The Carol Burnett Show" and a couple of shows that soared into oblivion, "The I Love TV Test" and "Alan King's

Third Final Warning." Both Gavin and I did several "Hollywood Squares" shows and Gavin appeared on "Password" with Ed Asner.

"It was the worst program in the history of the series," Gavin says now. "I'm just not a game person." But he appeared on other game shows: "Tattletales" with Bert Convy and "Celebrity Sweepstakes," just for the challenge.

I took care of everything at home. We had another new dog now, a Lhasa apso. He had an emotional disorder and bit anything that came near him. I said a little love would change all that. Ha! Muggsy remained a biter—another thing love alone could not change.

During one "Mary Tyler Moore Show" hiatus, Gavin wrote and directed *Are You Anybody?* with Lee ("Barnaby Jones") Meriwether and another play, *Madame Poncelli and the Indian Hoop Dancer of Ogden Utah* with Joyce Van Patten at the Theatre West in West Los Angeles.

He was nominated for a Golden Globe Award by the Hollywood Foreign Press Association as "Best Supporting Actor in a Comedy Series," but in spite of being busy and receiving worldwide attention, he was restless. He thought it meant he should work harder.

I asked him to slow down. Sometimes I'd want to go out to dinner or to a party. He would be too tired. He thought I was selfish—here he was, working ten hours a day, and I wanted to go partying when he was ready to collapse into bed at the end of the day.

When we were together, he'd fall asleep in the chair or on the sofa, and that would make me angry. He couldn't figure out what was wrong with me.

We stayed in Sherman Oaks for two and a half years, until the winter of 1976, and then we decided to buy that house in Palm Springs. We both loved Palm Springs. We enjoyed the casual, small-town atmosphere of the rich and not-so-rich, the sunshine, and the miles of endless blue sky. It was like an oasis in the middle of the frenzied, chaotic life in Los Angeles, where even quietness is permeated with anxiety.

Our Deepwell home was an adobe-style structure, typical of the desert, with cactus and jade plants growing all around, while the summer desert heat baked every tile and stone. It was peaceful and soothing to us both. We took long drives together, passing the homes of other celebrities who came to the desert for peace: Kirk Douglas on Via Lola, Lucille Ball on Club View Drive, Frank Sinatra on (what else?) Frank Sinatra Drive. The MacLeod house on Cactus Drive was too big for just the two of us. Kaye Ballard gave us a poodle we named Rose. She was the sweetest dog I've ever had—a person in a dog suit.

We had fantasized that our seven children—Gavin's four and my three—would visit often, and that we would be one big happy family, but that never happened.

Up until Gavin left me in 1981, it was his dream that he and his children would be reunited. I wanted that, too. We were always talking about the day we'd all be together, the two families, and everything would be happy and beautiful. But instead, we made a permanent hole in our dream.

In May 1981 we went to the Fiji Islands and Australia with "The Love Boat." I loved Australia and its people. They adored Gavin, and we were treated like royalty. Unfortunately, it was while we were in Australia that Gavin broke his ankle.

When we got home, Gavin went right into rehearsals for another show and opened in July in Florida. I landed a job of my own in a tour of *George M!* I had been hired for a show without Gavin! Ken Berry starred in the musical about the life of George M. Cohan. He and Brenda Thomson were terrific and the tour was perfect.

When I was out with *George M!* I went back to my room after the show, watched TV, or went out to eat. I'd talk to Gavin every night on the telephone, curled up in my robe in bed at the hotel. I thought, *Oh, I love my Gavin so much. I've got everything.*

But then I went to Florida to see my wonderful "Gavey" and came back devastated beyond belief. He was cold, indifferent. Uncaring. And only weeks before he had called me in Ohio, where the *George M!* tour was, and told my friend Donna Higgins, "The corn must be growing twice as high with my Sunshine there." He had sent me photos of a house he wanted to buy for us in Beverly Hills. He said he loved me! Now he was like a stranger.

I was so upset when I left Gavin, I don't know how I got to the airport. I was in a state of shock. I cried all the way to Los Angeles. A flight attendant was kind to me, helped me to a seat where I would have privacy, sat with me, brought me tea and magazines, and then when we got off the plane she helped me find a taxi. I loved her for helping me. I thought she was an angel of mercy.

But what an angel she turned out to be. The next thing I knew I was reading all about how I was having a total nervous collapse on the airplane and if it weren't for the help of the flight attendant, who was the heroine of the hour, I'd probably have committed suicide right in the aisle. She must have *run,* not walked, to the tabloids with her sizzling little story. I read it and it was yet another stab to the heart.

Then I received a letter from Gavin asking for a divorce.

Whatever lies were printed in the papers about us or Gavin were like love letters compared to the nightmare of that letter.

I stood in our living room on our hand-hooked turn-of-the-century rug with that piece of paper in my hand, my diamond sparkling above the word *divorce.* The sunlight was dancing on our beautiful antiques and collections of folk art. On the walls was only a partial display of our collection of primitive and naive paintings. I looked around our wonderful condominium with the panoramic view of the ocean and the Pacific Palisades, and I felt like the poorest, most desolate person in all the earth.

It was worse than anything I had ever had been through. It was worse than my father leaving us, worse than my mother's death, worse than my first divorce, worse than all my physical illnesses—it was *the worst.* It was pain twenty-four hours a day. There was no relief. I couldn't figure out why he left. I couldn't figure out how God could allow such an awful thing to happen. I couldn't figure out what was wrong with me.

A person who's never been rejected might not understand. I thought everything was fine. I thought we had a good marriage—from the perspective that *I* was holding it together. *I* was the one putting up with Gavin. All those years *I* had been tolerating *his* temper tantrums, *his* fits of anger, *his* selfishness, *his* overeating—and earlier in our life together, *his* drinking. I saw to it he took his vitamins; I was there in the morning with his juice and wheat germ. I took care of his laundry, his buttons, his dental appointments; I warmed his bed. I thought he loved me! I worked so hard to earn the right to be loved.

I told my story hundreds of times in the three years I was divorced from Gavin. I told it to newspaper and magazine reporters. I told it to television and radio hosts. I told it on the telephone and on platforms. I told it to friends, family, doctors—wherever I could. I helped form a group called L.A.D.I.E.S. (Life After Divorce Is Eventually Sane) for Hollywood wives whose husbands had left them. Women like Patti Lewis and Lynn Landon were active members. But getting famous because of suffering doesn't make fame or popularity desirable. I needed something to occupy my hours, days, and nights. Though he wasn't there, Gavin MacLeod was still the main character of my life.

The women in L.A.D.I.E.S. shared much of the same pain and the problems of adjusting to a life divorced from a celebrity. My entire life and life-style was thrown into a tailspin. I had been married to one of television's most successful actors. Now, as far as Hollywood was concerned, I was nothing, and I very much felt it. There was no more acclaim and attention; no more glamorous parties. I had to say good-bye to Aaron Spelling's and Doug Cramer's fabulous parties that both Gavin and I had loved. We were always invited to the most extravagant Hollywood events, and Gavin used to tell me with his marvelous grin, "It's like I always knew it would be on the other side of the tracks."

Now all that was over: dinners at which Doug would get Bobby Short to play and sing for us, even though he was just flying in from a long European tour. No more limos sent over to pick us up; no more fabulous beaded-gown events where I was Cinderella at the ball. No more fairytale life with the handsome prince.

But I lost more than the glamour. There was the sense of family with Gavin's co-workers and their wives and families. In show business you sometimes become closer to the people you work with than your own family. I would miss all that now because I was no longer family. I not only lost Gavin, I lost a world as well.

I had to start picking up the pieces. My friends and my children were worried about me. My health was rapidly going downhill and I was afraid I'd have another nervous breakdown.

In September of 1981 I began taking Singing on Stage classes with the wonderful David Craig in his studio on Hollywood Boulevard. This man literally saved my life. For those two hours in his class I became a sane person. I gained courage, confidence, and an actual sense of being okay. He was encouraging and understanding. I told him my life was falling apart, and with his characteristic wit and professionalism, he refused to allow me to give up.

Others in the class—Marcia Wallace, Frances Bergen, Howard MacGillan, and Steve Bulen—were so supportive and caring, it was as if we were teammates rather than classmates. These loving, talented people, including the incredible Gary Carver, David's long-standing accompanist, will forever remain close to my heart, which at that time they helped repair. David Craig arranged an audition for me for the part of Adelaide in *Guys and Dolls*.

Somehow I mustered up the courage to go, and amazingly enough, I got the job. It took me to Flagstaff, Arizona, where I worked hard rehearsing during the day and then went to my room and cried all night, missing my Gavin.

I dove into the numerology and astrology books. I needed help so desperately. My psychiatrist told me Gavin was the one with the problems. Friends told me to get him out of my system, kiss the marriage good-bye, get on with my life. At night I'd lie in bed and cry, "Why, God? Why?"

I loved and I hated Gavin. He had been saying, "I love you, I love you, I love you," and then with the same mouth he said, "I never want to see you again." I started thinking there was something wrong with *me*.

In our nine years together I thought it was me who did the putting-up-with, and it was me doing the silent suffering. I'd ask him nicely if he had called his daughter Julie. He'd scream back that Julie was *his* daughter and if he wanted to call her, he would. It was none of my business.

Gavin was saying I had been bossy and that I even commandeered our finances. I handled the money because I thought Gavin was a spendthrift. He'd go into an art gallery and buy whatever he wanted, and I'd go along with it, but we really couldn't afford to do that. So I put us on a budget, and we agreed we wouldn't buy another thing for a year.

When Gavin used to call me names and put me down, I didn't say anything because I was afraid if I did, he would walk out. I didn't want him to leave; I wanted an honest and open relationship. I wanted to talk to him and I wanted him to talk to me. I loved him. But he would blow up, fly into a rage, so I'd shut up. I was so afraid he'd tell me he wanted a divorce. I stopped expressing what I wanted. I really didn't know where to find help.

Gavin's secretary refused to let me through to him now. She guarded him like Fort Knox. I couldn't even talk to him.

The betrayal was so hard. Any woman who has ever been left by her husband knows what I'm talking about. One day you have plenty of friends. Then all of a sudden, the people you thought were your *best* friends are avoiding you, not answering your calls. I thought I was going crazy. Everywhere I went, people were buzzing about Gavin doing this, Gavin doing that, Gavin seeing this person, that person. They were *totally* uncaring toward me— I thought there was something terribly wrong with me.

In 1982 "The Love Boat" sailed to Athens, the Greek Islands, Istanbul, Monte Carlo, Capri, Rome, and Venice. Gavin told reporters, "I'm in touch with my soul; I've opened myself to change, to growth, to awareness."

I was able to follow Gavin's life through newspapers, magazines, and television. I read, as did the rest of the world, how he was no longer postponing life; he was, at the age of fifty-one, just beginning to live; he had only been incubating until now—and on "The Merv Griffin Show": "We had a wonderful marriage and then the laughs were over. It was time to move on, Merv. Color me a happy man."

Supposed friends were eager to let me know of Gavin's goings on and whereabouts; I heard blow-by-blow descriptions of his dates, where he partied and with whom, and whatever gossip scrapings friends and acquaintances might have overlooked, the media made up for.

1983 was another big year for "The Love Boat." Ratings soared. It was now seen in eighty-two countries of the world. It had taken over as the undisputed Saturday-night winner, clobbering the long-standing "Carol Burnett Show" right off the air. Gavin had rented a house in Beverly Hills before buying a home in Benedict Canyon. No businessman, he was spending money hand over fist. The "new," "free" Gavin was throwing his money away with such speed and alacrity, he didn't have time to ask questions about where it was going. There was the business of redecorating the house: new carpeting—four thousand square feet of it—landscaping, furniture, wallpaper.

A financial expert who had to be called in later esti-
mated that Gavin had frittered a fortune in the three years
of "being in touch with his soul." And looking back on it,
he wasn't even having a good time. I thought of him as
painfully and artlessly lost.

And I was lost. I was out of it. The bitterness and hurt
never, ever went away. Somebody told me I wanted Gavin
only for his money. I said, "I'm the only one who has *got*
his money. I've probably got more than he does." I was
extremely careful with that alimony.

Friends told me the house in Benedict Canyon was never
"finished." Workers, like ants, buzzed around the place
constantly, redoing, replanting, fixing, putting in something new, taking something out. You could practically
see the dollar bills flying out the windows and being hauled
away by the truckload. And I just knew he was probably
leaning on his kitchen counter, gobbling up Better Ched-
dars for breakfast, lunch, and dinner.

Meanwhile, I was traveling around the country appearing on television and radio with L.A.D.I.E.S. My friend Donna Higgins, who is like my sister, was especially helpful at this time. She stayed with me at the condominium. My Aunt Elsie, too, came to be with me for my son Tommy's wedding just two weeks after Gavin left. (Perfect timing.) Other friends tried to help me through the painful time following Gavin's departure.

Donna Higgins told friends that I cried nonstop for three years. "Patti," she said later, "was pretty much of a wreck. We didn't know if she'd ever snap out of it. Practically every sentence that came out of her mouth had Gavin's name in it. I knew Patti for a lot of years and never saw her so completely out of control. I had known her as a bubbling-over, effervescent-type person. But that was all gone when Gavin left.

"She and her L.A.D.I.E.S. group were good for each other because they could blow off steam together; they could get rid of anger and support one another. It was a first step for Patti to focus away from her pain. But even so, her mind was still centered on Gavin. She saw therapists, sometimes two or three times a week. She wanted help so badly, but she never felt she was getting help, because what she really wanted was Gavin. Nobody could bring her Gavin back home to her."

Now, I think Donna was right. I was running everywhere for help. I don't know how she stood living with me that year.

Then in February of 1982 I received a call from a woman named Edith Schaeffer. I had no idea who she was, but a mutual friend had suggested she call me.

"Could I come by for a few minutes?" The voice was gentle and unpretentious.

"Well, come on over then, Edith . . . sure." I wasn't so sure. Our mutual friend, Pat Colmenares, had been talking to me about Christ and about being Born Again.

The doorbell buzzed and when I opened the door, there in the shadows stood a simply dressed woman with a pleasant face, hair pulled back, strong, sharp features, and penetrating eyes. She wore a plain wool suit and carried under her arm a large, leather-bound Bible and a plain, no-nonsense purse. Standing on either side of her were two timid-faced women wearing slight smiles.

Edith Schaeffer, I was soon to discover, was not the sort of woman to mince words, play games, or be intimidated by anyone or anything. She had come there for one purpose: to lead me to the Lord. I hardly had a chance to offer the women a cup of tea before Mrs. Schaeffer was asking me if we might talk about a very serious matter in private. I was feeling nervous because Gavin was supposed to come over to get some things and I didn't know how I was going to handle that.

So this stranger took me into my back room, which was supposed to be a study but which I hadn't gotten around to fixing up since Gavin had left, and she put her arm around me and said, "My dear, dear Patti, God is reaching out to you with His love. . . ."

I broke down. Edith's voice was soft and reassuring: " 'Him that cometh to me,' Jesus said, 'I will in no wise cast out' [John 6:37]. Patti, the Bible says to believe on the Lord Jesus Christ, and you shall be saved" [Acts 16:31].

"I don't know what I need to be saved from," I moaned. "I'm so confused."

"Being saved, or salvation, is for the lost. If we could save ourselves, we wouldn't need a Savior. Jesus said, 'They that be whole need not a physician, but they that are sick' [Matthew 9:12]. Jesus said He came to call sinners to repentance" [verse 13].

"But I think I'm a good person. I try to live with certain principles, certain ethics—I'm honest, I'm fair, I don't try to hurt people. . . . If a clerk gives me too much change, I always point it out."

"Patti, you can't live as a so-called good person in your own strength. Nobody can. We meet with insurmountable obstacles; we have great limitations. If you want to be free of the unhappiness you bear, don't try to do it in your own power. The forces of evil are stronger than you are. Jesus is the One who makes us free. The Word of God tells us, 'If the Son therefore shall make you free, ye shall be free indeed' " [John 8:36].

"Edith," I replied, "I've tried all my life to follow the teachings of Christ . . . I've always believed that I *am* a Christian."

"First of all, trying is not what counts; it's *trusting*. You can paddle all you want out on the ocean trying to save yourself, but it's grabbing on to the lifeline thrown from the boat that will save you." Then she quoted from Scripture:

Behold, God is my salvation; I will trust, and not be afraid:
for the Lord JEHOVAH is my strength and my song; he
also is become my salvation (Isaiah 12:2).

"There's that word again: *salvation*. Edith, do I have to
be *saved?* Is that what I need?"

I prayed right there in my back bedroom with Edith
Schaeffer. Her quiet voice led and I followed: "Dear Jesus,
please come into my heart. Forgive me all my past sins,
take me as Your child to serve You, love You. . . ." The
words floated around my head like wafts of perfume. I
was becoming Born Again. It shocked me that I had never
really been a Christian. I had believed in Jesus, but I hadn't
really made Him and Him alone Lord of my life. It was all
a little clearer now.

Edith reached into her purse and pulled out some books
written by her husband. I looked at the name: Dr. Francis
Schaeffer. The books were called *The God Who Is There, The
Mark of the Christian,* and *No Little People.* Then she handed
me a small copy of the Gospel of John from the New
Testament in the Bible. "Do you have a Bible of your own?"
she asked.

Of course I had a Bible. I had everything: Bible, Tarot
cards, horoscopes, *The Book of Mao, Divine Health* by Mary
Baker Eddy, the Jewish Torah, *Zen,* A.A.'s *Twelve Steps,*
the *I Ching,* you name it. Edith convinced me to get rid of
everything except the Bible and good Christian books.

Soon it was time for her to leave. She had a plane to
catch, and I suddenly remembered how nervous I was
because Gavin was coming over. When she left, with the
two women moving noiselessly after her, I knew in my
heart that something spectacular had happened to me. I
promised Edith Schaeffer I'd read my Bible. I liked to keep
promises. I *would* read my Bible and I would pray.

Later that night, Gavin came through the same door looking, yes, just as everyone was saying: wonderful. He asked for a few things for his new place. I said (because I wanted to be so incredibly selfless and humble), "Gavin, you just go ahead and take whatever you need."

This was followed by sounds of the man I loved scuttering about my (our) condominium gathering up my (our) pictures, pieces of art, beautiful antique furniture, and as I sat in disbelief and heartbreak, he casually exclaimed, "Wow! This is fun!"

At that moment, the same woman who had given her heart, soul, and body to the Lord Jesus Christ in utmost sincerity just that afternoon felt tempted to push a man through a seventeenth-story window. There he was, whistling merrily while piling up our things by the door, as I stood with my eyes riveted to the window muttering, "No, don't even *think* it—it's a long drop—Patti, you'll get the *chair*."

I busied myself flying back and forth from Los Angeles to New York, auditioning for parts in plays. Each one brought a swarm of new terrors, the dread of getting up in front of the casting directors, displaying myself and my talents to be sawed asunder by indifference or an impassive, "Thank you very much—next!"

"Patti, why do you put yourself through such torture? *Why* do you want to be an actress?" my friends would ask.

I'd grunt ruefully, "Just a violent need for rejection, I suppose."

I knew something special had happened that day with Edith Schaeffer, but it wasn't until January of 1984 that I gave myself fully to the Lord to live His life through me, and I really *felt* God's closeness in my life. I attended prayer meetings with Patti Lewis. I had never heard people praying out loud before. One evening when it was time to take prayer requests, I blurted, "I have someone I want to pray for."

"Yes? Who is it?"

"I want to pray for my husband."

Nobody corrected me, "Your *ex*-husband, you mean—" I began to sob and the women gathered around me and held me. On and on they prayed, their voices like a warm blanket covering me. It was reassuring, a feeling that welled up from deep within, spreading over me. Yes, this was right, this was good. The women prayed, and I knew God was there and that He cared, and what's more, I knew and believed He was answering our prayers.

I seemed to feel better physically and emotionally. I stopped talking about Gavin so much. Instead, I was praying for him. My circumstances hadn't changed, but I changed.

I prayed every day for Gavin and for the restoration of my marriage. I contacted prayer groups to pray with me, including a group I was told about called Born Again Marriages. I became a regular member of Shirley (Mrs. Pat) Boone's Bible study in Beverly Hills.

Pray, pray, pray, that's what I did. And I read my Bible. I would sit in the living room in the early morning and start reading, and I'd read until it got dark. I *loved* the Word of God. I'd pray in the Spirit for Gavin, for me, for my children, and I'd pray in absolute faith that God was hearing my prayers. I could feel my whole body relax. I could feel myself calm down. I could feel myself changing.

My daughter, Stephanie, said my new faith made a difference in me. She felt I was more at peace. She told me later, "We were really worried about you, Mom, because all you did was talk about Gavin and you were so physically sick all the time. Then you seemed to get better after you became involved in your prayer group. You had made a commitment to God and it was obvious—sort of miraculous, really."

If I wasn't reading my Bible or praying, I was watching Christian television. I was developing favorites and wouldn't miss their programs, just as at one time I wouldn't miss a Betty Grable movie. It was the most exciting thing in the world for me to sit cross-legged on the sofa with my Bible, notebook, and pen on my lap, and watch Christian television. I figure in six months I got the equivalent of a year of Bible school. I discovered Christians were beautiful, loving, caring people, as well as fun. Everything was thrilling to me: the songs, the music, the gifts of the Holy Spirit, the love, the hugs, the sweetness of the people, and most of all, the new awareness of the love and presence of God.

My secular therapists had all told me to forget Gavin, let him go and get on with the business of living my life. My Christian friends and counselors were saying that the power of God could move mountains; that God is a God of restoration. The Bible says, "Ask and keep on asking; knock and keep on knocking" (see Matthew 7:7). I had so much confidence and faith when I prayed for Gavin. It was truly a privilege. And as I prayed, a new love for him developed in me. I began to love him more. I began to forgive him more.

The most amazing thing was happening: I began to like myself better. God was showing me I was worth something. He told me I didn't have to put myself down to justify a divorce. He showed me that in His eyes I was forgiven and righteous. I was His child, and that's what counted most.

The Lord was giving me strength I hadn't had before. My prayer partner, Louise French, told me not to be discouraged. I learned that my thoughts are subject to both the Lord Jesus and to the enemy (Satan). I wanted to think God's thoughts, so I began to pour God's Word into my mind every day. But even so, the enemy would nip at me with suggestions such as, "Are you going to spend your whole life praying for that jerk?" That's when I decided that even if Gavin did not come back to me, I would continue to pray for him and for his salvation.

My prayer, night and day, became that the Lord would heal my broken, seemingly hopeless marriage. "And please, dear Jesus . . . help me to be the person You meant me to be. And dear Jesus, bless Gavin right now wherever he is. . . ."

PART THREE

TOGETHER (AGAIN)

G

AVIN:

She looked so small there in the doorway. Was she always that *short?* I wondered. Her hair wasn't as blond as before, more brownish now. I liked it better blond. But her face was so cute, the way she looked in *The Chocolate Soldier* when she wore those bobbing yellow braids. "Hello, Patti. . . ."

I had always liked her hands. She had the tiniest fingers—narrow, tapered little fingers that made things look important when she touched them. Looking up at me, silent, smiling, she suddenly reached for me, and I folded my arms around her. Then her hand was in mine; she pulled me inside. Everything was so familiar. It was exactly as I knew it would be: neat, warm, welcoming. Patti always made a home a refuge. Why hadn't I realized that? All those houses we'd bought and decorated and purchased furniture and wallpaper for had been Patti's doing. She made even the dullest room into a cozy, happy retreat. I could smell dinner cooking. Candles lit the room.

"I hope you'll forgive me, Gavin," she said (and this

was her classic line told to one and all later), "your dinner is a little cold—it's been waiting three years."

"You look good."

"You, too."

We talked on—about a million things going on in our lives and in my work.

"You should have seen the *unreal* mosques or whatever they're called in Istanbul—I went to some strange religious ceremony one day, and the men were in one building, the women behind a wall in the back—"

"So the men don't become distracted by the women?"

"Yeah." I laughed. It had been three years, I realized, since we sat in the same room together. "It's been lonely without you."

"It's been lonely without you, too."

"The guy next door to me is suing me because when I bought that place the wall was two inches over onto his property."

"What?"

"Was I supposed to get out my measuring tape when I bought the place to check out every tree and shrub? Who does that?

"And I've got all this money going down the drain with that new production company. . . ."

"Let's play some of our old Jackie Gleason records."

"My mother has really been sick—"

"Let's tell funny stories—"

"Patti, I want you to know those things you've read in the newspapers aren't true. They're ridiculous—insane."

"Let's sing some Fred Astaire and Ginger Rogers songs—"

"Oh, Patti, it's so good to be with you. . . ."

"We could start with—*Pick yourself up, dust yourself off.* . . ."

I laughed softly, painfully, brushed the top of her head with the back of my hand. ". . . *start all over again.* . . ."

"Didn't you love that song? Remember Fred Astaire and Ginger Rogers had both fallen down when she was supposed to be teaching him to dance—"

"I remember you trying to teach me to tap dance a hundred years ago—"

"Something for everyone, it's comedy tonight—"

"Patti—"

"You were so good in that role, too, in *Forum*."

I laughed. We had dinner—nibbled at things is more like it—and talked and talked. Until the early morning. I fell asleep on the sofa. She dozed on the ottoman, curled up snaillike. I stretched and went to stare out the window at the pale light of morning just sneaking up on the ocean's edge.

"I've been lost, Patti—trying to find myself. . . ."

"I've prayed for you, Gavin," she told me.

I thought then it was just a manner of speaking. Not something real—with power.

"How about some tea?"

"Patti, please. Sit. I just want to talk to you."

She sat.

"You know, Patti, I always promised myself I would never be like my father and my grandfather. I promised myself I would always be happy. I've lost on both those counts. I promised I'd be a good father. Failed there. I promised myself I'd always have enough money and I'd never have financial problems again in my life. Failed on those counts—"

"Gavin, I don't know what to say except there is for-

giveness and love for you. There's a whole new life waiting for you."

My gaze dropped.

The teakettle whistled ready.

"I found a new life in Jesus! Oh, Gavin, it's wonderful.
Really."

I looked at her, smiled weakly, and sighed. I had tried
all the other religions, and they hadn't worked.

I looked around and felt a sense of comfort.

Everything was the same: the cupboards we had re-
placed with distressed barn wood, the ceramic hand-
painted tiles. An antique butter churn and other Early
American artifacts still lined the shelves and walls. The
same baskets hung from above the kitchen door frame on
an antique coatrack. She had such a flair for decorating
and collecting. I had missed that about her, too. Was that
why I suddenly felt so blasted *sad?*

She asked the big question: "Gavin, why did you leave
me?"

I hesitated, reached for her hand. She drew back. Her
feelings were showing. "I promise you, Patti, it wasn't for
another woman."

"But why did you leave?"

She could ask that question and I could try to answer
her, but I knew it wouldn't be adequate. Her questioning
only reflected her desperate wish for all the pain to be
gone. I wished I could give her an answer like a love song
in a play which was so powerful, so overwhelming, that
we both could throw back our heads and laugh, and forget
the last three years. But that's not real. And now she was
a Christian, a new person, she said. All things were new
and fresh and alive with hope and joy. She said she could
face reality without fear. She wasn't a victim any longer.

She was a child of God, not dependent on other people for her happiness. I wished I could have had the same confidence.

"Gavin," she told me, "since I gave my life to Jesus Christ, I experience His love and goodness every day. I really do. He helps me through the hard times. I wish I could explain it to you. . . ."

"I can see it," I told her. "I can see it in your eyes."

The tea was ready. We had it with the sun just coming up, shining through the ocean mist. I felt good; I wasn't even tired because inside I felt I was falling in love again with my ex-wife.

The September 15, 1981, issue of the *Star* ran a photo of Patti and me that had supposedly been taken in 1977. The headlines accompanying the photo read: GAVIN MACLEOD'S WIFE HEARTBROKEN AS LOVE BOAT STAR ENDS 7-YEAR MARRIAGE. The story indicated I was an uncaring phony who dumped his wife, justifying himself with words such as, "Enough is enough."

Three years and two months later, the *Star* ran the same photo in their November 6, 1984, issue with this caption: LOVE BOAT CAPTAIN GAVIN MACLEOD IS ALL SMILES NOW THAT HE'S LOST 34 POUNDS FROM HIS ONCE-TUBBY FRAME AND WON BACK HIS WIFE, PATTI. Subhead: PATTI WAS OBVIOUSLY HAPPY BEING BACK WITH HIM. I thought it was funny that I was able to lose thirty-four pounds in the same photograph.

The stories weren't always humorous. In July 1985, another weekly gossip paper ran a cover feature story on our remarriage: WE DIDN'T TELL OUR FAMILY—WE AREN'T SURE HOW THEY WILL REACT. There was a wonderful photo of my children, but the caption hurt me. KEPT IN THE DARK: MACLEOD DIDN'T TELL HIS FOUR CHILDREN ABOUT

THE SECOND MARRIAGE TO PATTI, WHO HAS THREE CHILDREN FROM
ANOTHER UNION.

The truth was, I did tell the children, but not the way I
should have. I really didn't know what to say. I simply
took Patti by the arm and showed up on my son Keith's
doorstep. "Look who's back," I announced merrily.

Perhaps Patti's and my reconciliation made my kids feel
they would see less of me. Maybe they felt they'd be put
in the background again and we'd share less activities together. My dream of one big happy family wasn't as sim-
ple as I always hoped it would be.

Still, ours was a happy recourtship. With Patti I could
laugh, play, sing, and feel good about myself again.

"I think you ought to go on Merv's show soon, Gavin,"
Patti said cheerfully one evening, as we sat together going
over my "Love Boat" lines, "and tell him the laughs are
here to stay."

I took her hand and held it. "I feel we're only just beginning now." Holding her hand lightly, I added, "I don't
know why, but I feel something fantastic is going to happen—"

Patti smiled. "Me, too."

How was I going to manage the enormous obstacles to
this reconciliation? I was learning that it's harder to rec-
oncile than it is to separate and get a divorce. It seemed
like everything was against it. Friends, family, the press,
being pulled a hundred ways at once in a hundred different directions—it was all exhausting. I had been dating
other people, and though the relationships were nonfulfil-
ling, I had to make explanations; I had the house in
Benedict Canyon to sell and there was moving, the finances, my mother's illness—I felt I was hanging on by
sheer willpower.

It was the ninth of October when Patti and I entered the Century Plaza Hotel in Los Angeles for a meeting of Born Again Marriages. The minister, Kent Axtell, talked about a verse I had heard a hundred times: "For God so loved the world, that he gave his only begotten Son, that whosoever believeth in him should not perish, but have everlasting life" (John 3:16). (And I thought I'd come to this service to hear something new.) Then the preacher spoke on another verse: "What is a man profited, if he shall gain the whole world, and lose his own soul?" (Matthew 16:26). "He that believeth on me hath everlasting life" (John 6:47).

I was restless. I remember thinking, *Now they're getting preachy. I'm really not in the mood for an Elmer Gantry scene.*

"For You, Lord, are good, and ready to forgive; and plenteous in mercy to all those that call upon You" (*see* Psalms 86:5).

Now I started to think. My mother had had a tumor on the left side of her brain the size of a baseball. I had sat beside her as she lay propped up in bed, her face distended, her eyes milky and dim. I had pleaded with God at the time: "Please heal her and *I'll do anything You ask. I'll live for You,* become a missionary—I'll give up acting—just don't let my mother die—please, God."

I started crying now. God had answered those prayers. *. . . whosoever believeth in Him should not perish, but have everlasting life.* What good would it do to be alive, I thought, if my own mother was in agony and without help? *What is a man profited, if he shall gain the whole world, and lose his own soul?*

Now the minister was talking about salvation through Jesus Christ. To my discomfort, Patti said, "Amen," every time the word *salvation* was mentioned.

Then the message was finished. The minister gave an

invitation for anyone who wanted Jesus Christ as the Lord of his life to step forward to the altar. To my immense surprise, I found myself rising from my seat as though an invisible hand had pushed me. It was as if I were broken inside—I wanted to give my life to God. I couldn't quench the sobs which surged up from the very depths of me. "Yes, I want You, Lord," I wept. "I am giving You my life."

I felt like a child again. I sensed barriers breaking down in me—barriers that had been there since I was a little boy in Pleasantville. I couldn't stop crying. Me, a grown man. I didn't know how badly I longed to trust something, how much I had wanted to belong to God.

The following evening Patti invited me to another meeting. She didn't have to persuade me to go. We met Shirley Boone and Kent and Dru Axtell and drove to Gary Greenwald's Eagle's Nest Church in Tustin. After a stirring message, the Reverend Sandy Brown called our group down in front for prayer. The voices of the praying people were like a sudden splash of scalding liquid. I jumped. Then I felt Shirley's hand on my shoulder, and she was praying for me out loud. The others joined. Then the minister chimed in and they were all praying at once with their hands on me. My knees buckled. It felt as if I were being pillowed to death. I wanted to resist; I felt angry and scared.

The only kind of prayer I was used to was a "Bless you" prayer. This was *work*. They were praying for my complete release from all my obsessions and fears, my release from the evil hold on my life.

What was happening was the fulfillment of the Scripture "We wrestle not against flesh and blood, but against principalities, against powers, against the rulers of the darkness of this world, against spiritual wickedness in high places" (Ephesians 6:12).

On the way home that night I told Patti I felt a hundred pounds lighter. Thank God for prayer, for the power of the Lord to free us from our invisible prisons, and thank God for loving Christians who care enough to pray. Later when I was alone, I opened the Bible to the Book of Psalms and read, "He shall call upon me, and I will answer him: I will be with him in trouble; I will deliver him, and honour him. With long life will I satisfy him, and shew him my salvation" (Psalms 91:15, 16).

I could almost hear Patti whisper, "Amen."

PATTI:
In the play *Mass Appeal*, Gavin played an older priest. Just before our second wedding he repeated the priest's last speech to me: "Up to now, my need for your love and approval has kept me silent and inactive. This is the first time I've ever said what I wanted to you. Only now is love possible. . . ."

As Gavin and I made our wedding plans, I felt that now love was possible. Now that we had said yes to the Author of love we could understand what it meant to be free from earning approval and craving it. Gavin and I never had enough approval. I now feel that the closer Gavin and I become to God, the closer we will be to each other.

We were in Omaha for a Born Again Marriage seminar when Gavin decided there couldn't be a better place or time to have the wedding. Pat and Shirley Boone flew in from California to be our best man and matron of honor.

"It was a storybook wedding," people told me, which really proves God planned it all. The wedding party wore pastel colors. ("No tribute to George Washington this time," I told reporters. "God is getting all the glory.")

I wore a soft blue silk dress and a garland of blue forget-me-nots and pink roses around my head and carried a matching bouquet. Pearl earrings and one strand of pearls around my neck completed my wedding outfit. Gavin was the handsome groom in his pale blue wool suit.

It all took place at the Red Lion Inn in Omaha. Gavin sang the praises of the inn, surely one of God's choicest havens on earth. It was the most beautiful place in the world, I felt, on that day, June 30, 1985. "They can have their Versailles, they can have their Egyptian Pyramids, they can have Windsor Castle, just give us the Red Lion Inn in Omaha," I told friends.

Chandeliers twinkled like billions of tiny smiling stars in the great lobby, off which was the grand ballroom where we tied the knot before a thousand people. Pat and Shirley Boone hurried in to find the wedding couple waiting, nervous and happy.

Pat sang "Just One More Chance" and "Amazing Grace," and Pat and Shirley sang a duet, "True Love." Gavin was in tears. He said, "I always cry at weddings, especially my own." He placed a tricolored gold wedding band next to the heart-shaped pink tourmaline and nine-diamond engagement ring on my finger. I became emotional and tearful when Kent Axtell asked us to state our vows in our own words.

"Patti," Gavin said, "I'm going to love you forever."

"Gavin, you are my love, my life."

There was hardly a dry eye during the communion service. The minister, Kent Axtell, talked about commitment to God and commitment to each other. We both felt that the Lord Himself was standing there whispering, "I love you, Gavin and Patti. I am pleased with you and I want you to live in My blessings and love from this time on."

Shirley Boone told me something special after the service. "You and Gavin show to us, the Church, and the world that God's power is not just there to forgive for past mistakes, but His grace is there to give us the power to live in forgiveness and love. He gave you and Gavin power to get through hard times, and that helps the rest of us."

Pat Boone was equally candid with Gavin. "Shirley and I have been married for thirty-three years," he told him, "and it has not been without problems. But we found out the Word of God works. Getting remarried isn't the end of something; it is the beginning of something. You have to work at marriage, and it starts with a relationship with the Lord." We both treasure their love and support.

While we stood on the platform, Gavin whispered lovingly, "Now I'll have to call you Patti MacLeod-MacLeod."

This time we didn't even mind what the tabloids said. One headline read: MACLEODS ARE HAPPY AGAIN. Another: LOVE BLOOMS AGAIN FOR LOVE BOAT SKIPPER AND EX-WIFE . . . THE MACLEODS ARE AFLOAT ONCE MORE.

We were. We are. We decided to work at it.

After the wedding we went on a fabulous cruise with "The Love Boat" to the Caribbean. It was wonderful. We went to the movies on board with Lana Turner, enjoyed a marvelous party dockside with Joan Collins, Morgan Fairchild, and Cary Grant, and "Captain Stubing" married Lana Turner and Stewart Granger.

The *Royal Princess* is one big, floating hotel. It has more than six hundred staterooms, a library, a theatre, night-clubs, discos, beauty salons, and a health spa with whirlpools, saunas, and enough exercise equipment to serve twelve hundred passengers. On this fabulous luxury liner, where romance is supposed to flourish beneath the blue skies of the Caribbean from Miami to Acapulco, Gavin and I spent our evenings listening to Christian teaching tapes in our stateroom. We had a great time, but I wonder what the other passengers thought when they heard, "Give *God* the *glory!*" and "Praise the Lord!" coming from behind our door.

There should be a "And they lived happily ever after" ending for a remarried couple. But even when the second honeymoon is over, there is the matter of readjusting, of relearning to live in a marriage that once went sour. We try to be open and candid with people about our relationship and about our lives as individuals.

G AVIN:
I'm fifty-five years old. Patti and I are both strong personalities. The demands of my career are hard on us. It's not all roses, but it's better than no flowers at all. We are trying to look at things as realistically as possible.

This is the best time of my life right now. I feel like a young person. I'm saved! These are glorious, free years. I feel in control because I have put the Lord in control. That takes a lot of the burden off me. These, at last, are the fun years. Patti and I laugh and talk and share and love.

I've always been concerned about the present. I used to tell people, "Live in the *now*." I think it's because when I was a little boy I wanted a life where I didn't have to worry. But now, I've got the answer to every problem that comes. I'm not dreaming and trying to escape through acting, or working, or drinking. With God's help I live life.

When Patti and I got back together I still could not deal with my feelings. I didn't want to make waves. I didn't want to deal with my emotions. Now I'm learning how to do that.

PATTI:

What I like is being Gavin's friend. I think now that we have given our lives and our marriage to God, we are able to be real friends, something we couldn't be before. Friends don't hurt each other and can confront and talk things out.

GAVIN:

In the past I felt Patti nagged me. Instead of dealing with my emotions, I would stuff them inside. On the outside I was smiling, my usual good-guy image, but on the inside I was in a rage. That's a terrible thing. I wonder how many other men do the same thing. I was like a stick of dynamite inside all the time. That's why I would explode over the smallest things.

Now God has given me a choice. I think happiness is a choice. There are people who have very little in life; they're very poor and yet they're happier than I was. There are people who are unhappy because they choose to be unhappy, even though they have all the money in the world.

A lot of people are searching and haven't found what they're searching for.

I used to equate beautiful houses with success. When I was a kid, we lived on the "other" side of the tracks. I thought everybody on the "other" side of the tracks had a more beautiful house than we did. I can still remember going to the other kids' homes to see the way they lived. If a person had a big house, I thought that person was happy. Now I know that God alone can give me happiness and security. *His* house is the only house that is important to me now.

When Patti and I got back together I sold the house in Beverly Hills and moved into the Santa Monica condominium. It was important for us not to be buying something or fixing something up because we needed time to concentrate on each other. When you're in the process of having your whole life restored to you as well as your marriage, you don't want to be busy doing a million other things.

PATTI:
I still have bitterness and hurt to work through. God restores relationships, but the healing may take some time. I need Gavin's assurance. Gavin was not abandoned, I was. Sometimes I still wonder how he could have walked out on me. Yet I believe God does a healing from the inside out, and that the healing takes time and hard work on my part. It takes a lot of loving help from a merciful God to heal such deep wounds.

Now that we're back together I have to really be careful that those old, bitter feelings don't remain in me. I have to face them, bring them out, and give them to the Lord. I have to pray, absorb the Word of God, and believe in what the Lord is doing *now*. Otherwise, I'll slip back into those hurt feelings that began way back when my father abandoned me. So you see, reconciliation isn't a bed of roses.

G AVIN:

For a long time I believed that Patti was the reason for my leaving the marriage. But God showed me that my priorities were all wrong. I had always thought my career was number one. I didn't realize I was a driven man; I didn't realize how stressed out and pressured I was in my work.

Now I realize there were moments with my children that I never had because I put my work first. There were moments I let slip through my fingers. My children grew up, and I lost out with them. If only I had been walking with the Lord, I would have had my priorities right and known that the family comes before my work. I guess I never really believed that there would be another job after the one I was working on was finished.

I used to say to myself when I was away from my family that if I were to die my children would probably write on my tombstone: ON THE ROAD AGAIN.

Now here I am, fifty-five years old and waiting for the next step God wants me to take. I'm absolutely confident in Him and overwhelmed with a sense of peace and security.

I have learned to see Patti with new eyes, to appreciate and love her as she deserves to be loved. At one time I saw her as an overbearing, pushy, and self-centered person. It takes hard work and commitment to the Lord to see with new eyes and a new heart.

PATTI:
Gavin and I love each other now more than ever before, yet it isn't the bells ringing, birds singing, fireworks-in-the-sky kind of thing where we're always ready to chase each other around the room night and day. It really ruffles my feathers when I watch television and see how love is portrayed for young people today. If you're looking for hype and stimulation every minute of the day, you're going to be disappointed. That's not what marriage is. Marriage is real life.

GAVIN:
The Lord showed me right away the parts of my life He was not pleased with. Before, I never thought there was anything wrong with me. That's what's so amazing. God is showing me how to think through reading the Word. I stopped telling off-color jokes completely. I stopped using certain language, the everyday kind of crude vocabulary that you think is okay after a while just because you're not using out-and-out filthy language.

I began praying night and day. We wake up in the mornings praying and thanking God for another day. We give ourselves to Jesus every single morning and ask in what way we can serve Him. It's wonderful. Invigorating! I feel like a kid when I talk about how wonderful the Lord is.

Our marriage had been broken, finished. But God healed it. Why would He heal our marriage just to watch it fall into a shambles again? He does the healing and He also gives us the grace to stay healed. It has taken some hard work and clear-cut decisions on both our parts, and it is going to continue to take our efforts to keep this relationship we have as fresh and beautiful as it is today.

Since making our commitment to Jesus and to each other, Patti and I have stood before many audiences telling what God has done in our lives. We've appeared on Christian television and radio programs, and evangelists have invited us to take part in their services as well as be a voice in their ministries. On television we have been given the privilege of hosting the "700 Club" program for Pat Robertson; we've appeared with Jim and Tammy Bakker on the "PTL Club," and have been interviewed by Jan and Paul Crouch on the Trinity Broadcasting Network. Christian magazines have bombarded us with requests for feature stories and articles. We would be worn out were it not for the loving care of our prayer partners and Christian friends.

In March 1986, the cast of "The Mary Tyler Moore Show" attended and paid tribute to Mary on the "Television Hall of Fame" awards ceremony in Santa Monica. It was Old Home Week for us as we talked and laughed and shared stories, catching up on one another's lives.

Ted Knight had undergone surgery earlier to remove a cancerous growth, but the cancer was back and had visibly weakened him. He had finished the arduous taping of twenty-two shows for his hit series "Too Close for Comfort," but didn't renew his contract.

Shortly after, Patti and I went to visit Ted. We told him what the Lord had done in our lives. He listened and said, "If He got *you*, Gavin, He can get anybody." Ted and Dottie prayed with us and gave their hearts to the Lord.

"You're Born Again now, Ted," I whispered into his ear. "You're going to heaven."

"I'm going to heaven . . ." Ted repeated.

Patti and I were appearing in the play *Never Too Late* in Cape Cod when Ted died. I was asked to give the eulogy and with my heart in my throat, remembering back to 1957 when Ted and I first met, I penned it in letter form. Here is a little of what I said:

> Dear Ted,
> . . . Patti and I cried rivers of tears when we heard the news, but forget our mourning. I want to celebrate your life. I want to thank you for having shared your entire being, not only with me but with the world. If laughter is healing, think how many millions you helped heal. That alone is tribute enough for any ordinary mortal, but you were far from ordinary, Ted. . . .
>
> You were blessed with success in all areas of your life. But your two Emmys, all your accolades and awards, pale in comparison with the award you received the last time we were together, just a few weeks ago, when you asked Jesus to come into your life. Because of this, we know where you are at this very moment. You are in our Father's arms and if I know you, Ted, the angels are smiling their biggest smiles ever. You have finally done it all. . . .

I met Dr. Ed Cole, the founder of Maximized Manhood, when I guest hosted the "700 Club" in April of 1986. Ed told me, "I'd like to see you in another series when 'Love Boat' ends." (I had been wondering if the Lord wanted me to quit show business and go into the ministry.)

Ed said, "I believe God has called you to the entertainment world, Gavin. Just be the best actor you can be for Jesus."

Our pastor, Jack Hayford, of the Church on the Way in Los Angeles, knew Patti and I were people in pain when we started attending his church. "Now there is such a

beautiful evidence of the Lord working in your lives," he
marveled. "Only the grace of God could have erased your
pain; it's a testimony to the miracle power of God."

Patti and I can believe in miracles now. We're building
our lives around a miracle. And we're working at "happily
ever after."

GAVIN AND PATTI'S TEN RULES FOR A "HAPPILY EVER AFTER" MARRIAGE

1. **Pray Together Every Day.** Every morning we have devotions *together*. Our personal prayer time with the Lord is our own responsibility, and we take our separate time for that alone each day, but our together devotional time is absolute priority. We follow a monthly devotional that includes a Bible portion which we read out loud. We talk about it and then we pray out loud, taking turns. We have a prayer list which we cover every single day, starting with our children. We try not to let anything interfere with this special and vital time. Everything during the day will be touched by those precious moments we spent in the presence of the Lord together first thing in the morning.

2. **Discuss Feelings and Desires.** We don't hold back now. We are able to share and keep our communication wide open. When we clam up or don't talk, we take a giant step backwards; we pull away from love. We want to move *toward* love, not away from love.

3. **Don't Try to Change Each Other.**   We have given each other the right to have feelings and opinions and ideas that differ. We have decided to love each other as we are today, right now, just as God loves us. This is so important because it frees us to feel okay about ourselves.

4. **Don't Treat the Present as if It Were the Past.** Sometimes it is easy for us to slip into the negative patterns we built up in our first years together. Then we'll imagine what is going on today is a repeat of yesterday. It's really important to recognize that we are new creatures in Christ Jesus. Every day we tell ourselves that. It's wonderful. Every day can be a refreshing and invigorating surprise when you see yourself in this light. The past is over! This is a *new* day.

5. **Don't Become Separated for Long Periods of Time.** Since we've been remarried, we have had opportunities to go work at jobs that would separate us for weeks or months. Instead, we chose to work together. But you can be apart when you're under the same roof fifty-two weeks a year, too. You can come home from work each day and not really take time for each other. You can become busy with life and leave each other out. A smile and a meal together isn't enough, especially when you're *restoring* a relationship. We want to be in the process of *building* our marriage into the best one we can, and if we don't take time for each other, we will wind up in the same alienated predicament we were before.

6. **Don't Allow Other People to Separate You.** When you're remarried, people may tend to still view you as single. There may be favorites played. We go places *together*. We meet friends *together*. We make decisions *together*. We want to be very wise in this area, so we have friends *together* and are established

as a couple; not "Gavin MacLeod and his wife" but "Gavin and Patti MacLeod."

7. **Be Sensitive to the Other Person.** God sees us as *partners*, not as master and slave. We have promised each other, "Your wants and needs are as important as mine." It's wonderful.

8. **Don't Demand the Other Be Strong and Perfect at All Times.** When one of us is low, the other doesn't fall apart. We take up the slack. We intercede in prayer for each other and for the situation. We don't demand one another to be 100 percent perfect at all times just because we're Christians.

9. **Give Each Other Space.** Don't try to possess or control the other person or patrol your mate's actions. Love each other and then set each other free. That's *trust*.

10. **Reaffirm Your Commitment Daily.** Wrap these ten steps in the majesty of God and the Holy Spirit, and you have something more beautiful than we can describe. The imperfections are nothing because your commitment to God is so great, your love for Him so strong and good. The things that at one time sent you running for the nearest door now won't even faze you. This is the miracle-working love of the Lord.

OTHER BOOKS BY MARIE CHAPIAN

Biography:

Help Me Remember . . . Help Me Forget
  (previously titled *The Emancipation of Robert Sadler*)
Of Whom the World Was Not Worthy
Escape From Rage
Forgive Me (with Cathleen Crowell Webb)

Christian Living:

Love and Be Loved
Staying Happy in an Unhappy World
Growing Closer
Telling Yourself the Truth (with William Backus)
Why Do I Do What I Don't Want to Do?
  (with William Backus)
Free to Be Thin (with Neva Coyle)
There's More to Being Thin Than Being Thin
  (with Neva Coyle)
Slimming Down and Growing Up (with Neva Coyle)
Fun to Be Fit